What Tribe of Israel Am I From?

By

Prophetess Mary J. Ogenaarekhua

Endorsements

"Prophetess Mary Ogenaarekhua is uniquely gifted in 'rightly dividing the Word of Truth.' She has a sharp discerning mind to negate any false doctrines that are circulating in the body of Christ and to set the record straight. This is what we need in these last days. I have great confidence in the revelations that she receives from the Lord and the 'Rhema' Word of God which is a great priority in her life. This book is a must read for any son or daughter of God who seeks the absolute truth concerning our relationship to our Jewish Roots and to live accordingly."

–Deborah Mordecai

Dedication

I dedicate this book to God the Father, God the Son and God the Holy Ghost. Lord God, You gave me the words to write in this book and I thank You for also giving me the grace to do it. As it is written in **Psalm 68:11**, so You have done concerning this book:

> *"The Lord gave the word: great was the company of those that published it."*

Thanks Father for teaching me how to hear Your voice for anything that I desire to know about You, About Your Son, about Your Holy Spirit and about your kingdom. Thanks for also using me to teach others. It is a great honor to have You as my Father and my Teacher. May this book bring You glory in Jesus name.

I also dedicate this book to all those who want to know the tribe of Israel that they are from. I hope that it answers all your questions.

What Tribe of Israel Am I From?

Unless otherwise indicated, all scriptures are quoted from the King James Version of the Bible.

Published by: **To His Glory Publishing Company, Inc.**
463 Dogwood Drive, NW
Lilburn, GA 30047
(770) 458-7947
www.tohisglorypublishing.com

This Book is available at:
Amazon.com, BarnesandNoble.com, Booksamillion.com, Canada, UK, Australia, etc.

Also, see the Order Form at the back of this book or call/email below to order this book.

Email: tohisglorypublishing@yahoo.com
(770) 458-7947

ISBN: 978-0-9821900-6-7   or   0-9821900-6-9

Table of Contents

Preface

This book is designed to answer the questions of some Christians who are trying to determine the tribe of the natural Israel that they are from. The reason they want to know this is because there are some teachings going on in Christendom in which Christians are being assigned to the various tribes of Israel. As a result of what is going on, I decided to address this issue in this book so that we can all see how Christians fit into God's plan concerning the natural tribes of Israel.

This book does not represent any of my church membership, affiliations and associations. Also, I have not written this book to devalue or belittle any of the tribes of Israel but rather to explain how Christians fit into the Jewish tribes. As born again Christians adopted by God in Christ Jesus, we are now partaking of the Abrahamic Covenant Blessings. <u>What this means is that we are now Jewish by adoption</u>. Therefore, I place a great value on Israel and its natural tribes.

I wrote this book as instructed by God and I hope that those who have ears to hear will hear the Lord's voice as they read it.

— Dr. Mary J. Ogenaarekhua

Acknowledgements

I thank God Almighty for inspiring me to write this book. Thanks Father for calling me to rise up and write what You showed me concerning Your house (the Church) and some of the teachings that are going on in it. Writing this book was truly a call to action and I give You all the glory in Jesus name.

I also want to thank all those who shared with me about their assigned tribes. I appreciate your concerns and your desire to know the truth about Christians and the 12 tribes of Israel. God used you all to help motivate me to get to work on this book so thanks for helping to make the writing of this book possible.

Chapter 1
The Blessings of
the 12 Tribes of Israel

God is Not a Respecter of Persons

Before we determine the tribe of Israel that you are from as a born again Christian, we have to first take a closer look at why it may at times seem to us that God blesses one person over another. The reason I am telling you this in the very beginning is because each of the 12 sons of Jacob received a very unique blessing from their father Jacob. As you read the blessings outlined in **Genesis 49**, you will immediately notice that these blessings are not equal. Some of the sons of Jacob did not receive a blessing at all.

Therefore, we have to first of all be well grounded in the understanding that God does not favor one person over another or bless or reward one person over another person without any reason. **What He does is reward whoever deserves it.** In other words, He rewards those who do well by His standard. The same is true when it comes to the blessings that He released through Jacob to his 12 sons.

Meaning, the patriarch Jacob was under God's anointing when he released the blessings to his 12 children which later became known as the 12 tribes of Israel. The blessings were released according to the will of God. This is the reason we need to know up front that God is no respecter of person.

Jacob's Blessings on His 12 Children

When Jacob became aware that it was time for him to depart from this world, he called his 12 sons together so that he can pronounce the word of the Lord over them before he died. We refer to those words today as **the blessings of the tribes of Israel or the tribal blessings** and they are found in **Genesis 49:1-27**:

> "And Jacob called unto his sons, and said, **Gather yourselves together, that I may tell you that which shall befall you in the last days.** 2 Gather yourselves together, and hear, ye sons of Jacob; and hearken unto Israel your father."

Jacob can only tell his children what would befall them in their last days by the help of the Spirit of God that was guiding him. Otherwise, he cannot know this by himself. This is why we can safely say that he was under God's anointing when he spoke the blessings over his children.

Differences in the Blessings of Each Tribe

As I stated in the preface, there is a new teaching going on concerning the tribes of Israel in the Church of Jesus Christ today and different Christians are now being told that they belong to the different tribes of Israel. As a result of this new teaching, many Christians are being assigned to different tribes.

The effect of this new teaching is that there are now a lot of Christians that are currently wondering about the tribe of Israel that they are

from. The reason this is important to them is because as I stated earlier, when you look at the blessings of the different tribes, you will see that not all the tribes received the same type of blessing.

Some of the blessings seem to be better than others while some seem to be harsh judgments for past transgressions. For example, **Simeon** and **Levi** did not receive any blessing and **Reuben actually received a curse instead of a blessing** because he slept with one of his father's concubines. We see this in **Genesis 49:3-7:**

> **"Reuben, thou art my firstborn, my might, and the beginning of my strength,** the excellency of dignity, and the excellency of power: 4 <u>Unstable as water, thou shalt not excel;</u> because thou wentest up to thy father's bed; then defiledst thou it: he went up to my couch.

> 5 **Simeon and Levi are brethren;** <u>instruments of cruelty are in their habitations</u>. 6 **O my soul, come not thou into their secret; unto their assembly,** <u>mine honour, be not thou united</u>: **for in their anger they slew a man, and in their selfwill they digged down a wall.** 7 <u>Cursed be their anger, for it was fierce; and their wrath, for it was cruel: I will divide them in Jacob, and scatter them in Israel."</u>

If you are assigned to the tribes of Simeon or Levi, you will have a cause for concern because when you pray to God to bless you, I do not believe that what is pronounced on these tribes is what you had in mind! Jacob basically rejected both Simeon and Levi and he did not even want his memory (honor) to be associated with them after his death.

Also, we must be aware that **not all the tribal blessings are eternal.** In other words, **not all the blessings that each tribe received have the provision for <u>eternal life</u>.** You see examples of this in **Genesis 49:19-21** concerning the blessings that **Gad, Asher** and **Naphtali** received:

> "**Gad,** <u>a troop shall overcome him</u>: but he shall overcome at the last. *20* **Out of Asher** <u>his bread shall be fat</u>, and he shall yield royal dainties. *21* **Naphtali** <u>is a hind let loose</u>: he giveth goodly words."

As you examine these three tribal blessings above, you do not see any provision for eternal life in any of their blessings. Now, when you look at **Genesis 49:9-12** and you see the blessings that Jacob pronounced over **Judah,** you will agree with me that all the blessings are not equal and that they do not all have provisions for eternal life.

> "Judah is a lion's whelp: from the prey, my son, thou art gone up: he stooped down, he couched as a lion, and as an old lion; who shall rouse him up? *10* **The sceptre shall not depart from Judah,** nor a lawgiver from between his feet, <u>until Shiloh</u> come *(Shiloh is the Jewish name for the*

Messiah); **and unto him shall the gathering of the people be.**

11 **Binding his foal unto the vine, and his ass's colt unto the choice vine; he washed his garments in wine, and his clothes in the blood of grapes:** 12 **His eyes shall be red with wine, and his teeth white with milk."**

An analysis of **Judah's blessings** reveals that they are quite different from the blessings that **Gad, Asher** and **Naphtali** received; not to mention the blessings that **Reuben, Simeon** and **Levi** received. Again, you have to remember that when Jacob was pronouncing these blessings, he was under the anointing. Therefore, we have to examine how God presided over how the blessings were given out from one generation to another. Because this knowledge is critical to the point that I am making, which is that God is not a respecter of persons. I will take you through this process in the scriptures in the next chapters.

Chapter 2
How God Watched Over
the Messianic Blessings

Although each tribe received a word from Jacob, what you will discover is that God has been watching over a particular blessing through several generations to make sure that it was delivered into the right hand in each of those generations. God's diligence over this matter began in the Garden of Eden right after Adam and Eve rebelled against Him by disobeying His Word. God immediately killed a lamb and covered Adam and Eve with the blood and the skin of the lamb. I will discuss the significance of this act by God in detail a little later in this chapter.

What I want you to be aware of right now is that **in killing a lamb as an offering for sin, God instituted a system or method of atonement that Adam began to practice.** In other words, Adam began to offer <u>a blood sacrifice</u> to God from time to time. It is not clear if Adam knew that it was a form of atonement for sin but what we know is that his children; especially Abel learned it from him.

Cain's Sacrifice is Rejected by God
Adam and Eve produced two sons named **Cain** and **Abel** and both of them had watched Adam offer blood sacrifice to the Lord as they were growing up. When they became adults, it was now their turn to bring their sacrifices to the Lord. In line with what he had seen his father do, Abel brought **a blood sacrifice** but Cain

in a rebellious state brought **a grain sacrifice.** Therefore, God said NO to Cain's grain sacrifice and He accepted Abel's blood sacrifice. From God's **rejection** of Cain's **grain sacrifice,** we can deduce that God was aware that Cain knew what type of sacrifice to bring. God would not have rejected Cain's offering if Cain did not know the type of offering that God required.

> **"And in process of time it came to pass, that Cain brought of <u>the fruit of the ground</u> an offering** *(grain sacrifice)* **unto the LORD.** *4* **And Abel, he also brought of the <u>firstlings</u> <u>of his flock and of the fat thereof</u>** *(blood sacrifice).* **And the LORD <u>had</u> <u>respect unto Abel and to his offering</u>:**
>
> *5* **<u>But unto Cain and to his offering he had not respect.</u>** **And Cain was** very wroth, and his countenance fell. *6* And the LORD said unto Cain, Why art thou wroth? and why is thy countenance fallen? *7* If thou doest well, shalt thou not be accepted?" (Genesis 4:3-7).

As you can see, God accepted Abel's sacrifice but rejected Cain's. **What Cain did not realize about God's requirement for a blood sacrifice of a lamb was that the sacrificed lamb was a type of Christ.** It spoke to the coming of the Messiah who will give His life as a lamb sacrificed for the sin of the world.

God was using the act of sacrificing a lamb to

teach man (beginning from Adam) about the ultimate sacrifice that was coming. This is why when John the Baptist saw the Lord Jesus; he immediately testified that Jesus was God's lamb to be sacrificed for the sin of the world in **John 1:29**:

> "The next day John seeth Jesus coming unto him, and saith, **Behold the <u>Lamb of God</u>, which taketh away the sin of the world.**"

To make his rejection worst, Cain again disqualified himself through his willful act of disobedience to God's word that he should do better next time by committing a grievous sin. Rather than obey God, he killed his brother Abel out of jealousy because God accepted his offering. With Abel gone, there was no lineage for the righteous because Cain had sealed his choice of rebellion by killing his brother. Therefore, God waited for Adam and Eve to produce another son called **Seth**. Through Seth, God can again begin to watch over the lineage of the righteous to bring forth a Messiah.

Abraham is Chosen

The descendants of Seth reproduced over many generations and populated the earth. When it was time for God to choose a man on earth to work through in order to bring about His plan of redemption for man, we learned in **Genesis 12** that He found a man named **Abram**. He made a promise to this man about giving him a son and He made the man to wait 25 years before manifesting the promise to him.

Abram was 75 years old when God spoke to him about giving him a son and Abraham believed God and God counted it to him as righteousness because he believed God. Then God made a covenant with Him and declared that through this man that He renamed **Abraham,** "shall all the families of the earth be blessed." Again, God is speaking about the coming of the Messiah.

> "Now the LORD had said unto Abram, Get thee out of thy country, and from thy kindred, and from thy father's house, unto a land that I will shew thee: 2 And I will make of thee a great nation, and I will bless thee, and make thy name great; and thou shalt be a blessing: 3 And I will bless them that bless thee, and curse him that curseth thee: **and in thee shall all families of the earth be blessed**" (Genesis 12:1-3).

Remember what I said earlier that God is no respecter of persons but He rewards the person that deserves it, we see this demonstrated in His dealing with the man **Abraham**. God needed to test Abraham to make sure that he qualified for what He wanted to do through him. Therefore, God requested that the child (Isaac) that Abraham waited 25 years to have be sacrificed by Abraham to Him!

> **"And it came to pass after these things, that God did <u>tempt</u> Abraham, and said unto him, Abraham: and he said, Behold, here I am. 2 And he said, Take now thy son, <u>thine only son</u>**

Isaac, whom thou lovest, and get thee into the land of Moriah; and offer him there for a burnt offering upon one of the mountains which I will tell thee of" (Genesis 22:1-2).

In obedience, Abraham took his son **Isaac** to Mount Moriah to sacrifice him on the altar that he had built there. Abraham had faith in God's abilities and he was fully persuaded that even if God made him to kill his son Isaac, God was able to raise the child up again from the dead. Therefore, Abraham proceeded to sacrifice his beloved Isaac but before Abraham could strike his son with a deadly blow, God called out to him in **Genesis 22:15-18**:

"And the angel of the LORD called unto Abraham out of heaven the second time, 16 And said, By myself have I sworn, saith the LORD, for because thou hast done this thing, and hast not withheld thy son, thine only son: 17 That in blessing I will bless thee, and in multiplying I will multiply **thy seed** as the stars of the heaven, and as the sand which is upon the sea shore; and **thy seed** shall possess the gate of his enemies; 18 And in **thy seed** shall all the nations of the earth be blessed; **because thou hast obeyed my voice**."

As you can clearly see in the scriptures above, God tried the man Abraham and Abraham obeyed God and God rewarded Him for his obedience. Why is God doing this? God wanted a man who will obey

Him so that God can manifest His salvation plan for humanity through him. <u>If Abraham had not passed the test, he would not have received the blessing</u>.

The reason that God had to go through this much trouble is because there is a sin problem between man and God and God wanted to deal with the sin problem in the world. He needed a man on earth to act on His behalf because He gave the earth to the children of men through Adam. Therefore, in order for Him to save man, He had to find a way into the earth realm through a man so that He can personally deal with the problem of sin Himself.

His plan is to come through the person of the Messiah known as the Lord Jesus Christ; **the seed that God spoke about in Genesis 22**. The Apostle Paul confirms for us in **Galatians 3:16** that the seed that God spoke to Abraham about was Christ:

> **"Now to Abraham and <u>his seed</u> were the promises made. He saith not, And to seeds, as of many; but as of one, And to <u>thy seed, which is Christ</u>."**

Again, the reason that I am telling you all these things is because I want you to see how from the very beginning, God began to watch over this particular blessing that came on Judah. God started watching over how the blessing was passed on beginning with Cain and Abel and later with Esau and Jacob; the sons of Isaac. Remember that God made the covenant blessing with Abraham and with Abraham's

28

seed. Abraham had two sons and one was named Ishmael and the other was named Isaac.

Isaac is Chosen

Although Ishmael was Abraham's first son, he was born to Abraham by an Egyptian concubine or servant and not by Abraham's legitimate wife Sarah. Isaac was born to Abraham by Sarah his legitimate wife when she was 90 years old. From this you can see that God honors the family unit that He instituted in the Garden of Eden between Adam and Eve. Therefore, He chose Isaac as the legitimate heir of the Abrahamic Covenant Blessings. He told Abraham that his seed shall be chosen from Isaac and not Ishmael.

"Of whom it was said, **That in Isaac shall thy seed be called...**" (Hebrews 11:18).

What this means is that the Messiah shall come through lineage of Isaac and not Ishmael. If you look again at the scriptures in **Genesis 22:2** and **Genesis 22:6**, you will see that God referred to Isaac as Abraham's only son! **Ishmael was not even considered by God because he was illegitimate.** True to God's Word, Isaac married Rebekah and she finally got pregnant when she was forty years old and they had twins; Esau and Jacob.

What is interesting is that when Rebekah was pregnant, the boys in the womb were already fighting. She was troubled because of the warfare that was going on inside her womb so she went to see a man of God (a prophet) about it. She was told the following in **Genesis 25:23**:

> "And the LORD said unto her, <u>Two nations are in thy womb, and two manner of people shall be separated from thy bowels</u>; and <u>the one people shall be stronger than the other people</u>; and **the elder shall serve the younger.**"

When you look at the above scripture, you notice that God has just done something unusual. He set the younger over the elder and according to our human concept of fairness, we would say that God has just been unfair. Again, remember that God is no respecter of persons therefore we will discover in the next chapter why God did what He did between Esau and Jacob. I will talk about the two in detail in the next chapter. Also, this scripture above will later help you to understand why Rebekah helped Jacob and not Esau when it came time for the boys to receive the Abrahamic Covenant Blessings.

Chapter 3
How Did God Choose Between Esau and Jacob?

We have already seen that **Esau** and **Jacob** were the children of Isaac and that Isaac was the custodian of God's covenant blessings; he inherited the blessings from his father Abraham. **Even before they were born, God foresaw that Esau would be of no use to Him because of Esau's profane nature** *(had no appreciation for something sacred such as his birth right)* and his rebellious actions. According to **Genesis 25:28-34**, Esau on a whim sold his birth right to Jacob his brother:

> "And Isaac loved Esau, because he did eat of his venison: but Rebekah loved Jacob. 29 And Jacob sod pottage: and Esau came from the field, and he was faint: 30 And Esau said to Jacob, Feed me, I pray thee, with that same red pottage; for I am faint: therefore was his name called Edom. 31 <u>And Jacob said, Sell me this day</u> thy birthright.
>
> 32 **And Esau said, Behold, I am at the point to die: and what profit shall this birthright do to me?** 33 **And Jacob said, Swear to me this day; and he sware unto him: and he sold his birthright unto Jacob.** 34 Then Jacob gave Esau bread and pottage of lentiles; and he did eat and drink, and rose up, and went his way: thus Esau despised his birthright."

God dislikes people who treat the holy and the sacred things of God as though they are nothing. When you compare Esau's action to that of Naboth who was killed by Jezebel (King Ahab's wife) because he refused to sell his inheritance to King Ahab in **1Kings 21:7-26**, you will see how God reacts to those who know the value of what He has given them. God avenged Naboth's death by sending Jehu (Captian of the Host of Israel's army) to destroy King Ahab's house along with his wife Jezebel. God did this for Naboth because Naboth unlike Esau knew the value of his inheritance. God will not give His blessing to those who do not value it.

Today, Esau single handedly represents such people in scriptures. He was not only profane but was also rebellious in nature. It is good to always remember that obedience is very important to God because He hates rebellion. He looks for a man that will always obey Him but Esau was not such a man.

Esau saw no value in his birthright but Jacob did. By the time Esau realized the value of his birthright, he had already given it away. He cried for his father to undo what was done but his father could not. His father told him that he cannot withdraw the blessing from his brother Jacob and that he had forever made Esau a servant to his younger brother Jacob. **Hebrews 12:16** also tells us that when Esau realized what he had done, it was too late for him.

> **"Lest there be any fornicator, or profane person, as Esau, who for one morsel of meat sold his birthright.** *17* For ye know how that afterward, when he would have

inherited the blessing, he was rejected:
**for he found no place of repentance,
though he sought it carefully with tears"**
(Hebrews 12:16-17).

Esau did what God has been carefully trying to teach
man not to do — toss out what we receive from Him
because we view it as worthless. In summation, we can
say that Esau was both rebellious and profane and as
a result, God had to reject him. God saw that Esau was
"no good" and that he would not be of any use to Him
in His plan of salvation. He was not reliable and so
cannot be counted upon to make godly decisions.

**God tries to avoid a repeat performance of what
Adam did in the garden because God gave the title
deed to the whole world to Adam in the Garden of
Eden but Adam gave it away to the devil. Therefore,
God wants to avoid those who will do a similar thing
in the future concerning His plan of salvation.**

You also need to remember that the scriptures
inform us in **Psalms 58:3** that the wicked are
estranged from the womb. What this means is that
God saw Esau from the womb.

**"The wicked are estranged from the
womb: they go astray as soon as they be
born, speaking lies."**

When you read about Esau, what you will see is that
Esau loved to do whatever his parents did not like. The
first thing he did was to marry the daughter of Ishmael
(Abraham's son) just to vex his parents and when he
overheard his parents telling Jacob not to marry a

Canaanite woman, he in defiance of them went and took a Canaanite woman as his second wife. He was not the type of person that God could give anything of value such as the lineage of the Messiah.

Jacob is Chosen

Because of Esau's profane ways, God chose Jacob even from the womb as the one who would inherit the Abrahamic Covenant Blessings. As it is written in **Romans 9:13,** God said before the kids were even born:

> "**Jacob have I loved,** but **Esau have I hated.**"

Hate is a pretty strong word and God spoke this before the boys were born. Why will God hate one and love the other? We saw the answer to this question in the discussion about Esau and **we will do well to always remind ourselves that God tries the hearts of men; even in the womb!** We have already seen in the previous paragraphs that the boys were fighting in the womb. When God looked at them, He knew exactly what was going on; He saw Esau's character even as he fought with his brother in the womb.

Again, before God gives something like the lineage of the Messiah to a person, He had to be sure of the character of the person. **Also remember that He sees the end from the beginning** as stated in **Isaiah 46:10.** This is why He can say, "I hate Esau but I love Jacob." He already saw Esau making trouble even in the womb. I say again that He knew that Esau was not going to be of any use to Him because Esau had a profane nature; he had no regard for things that are sacred. We saw how Esau gave away his birth right without a second thought.

Jacob on the other hand was not a perfect man when you read about him and some of his ways but the one thing that you can count on him for is a healthy respect for the things of the Lord. He saw right away the importance of the birth right and went after it. He could have bargained with his brother Esau with some other item but he chose the birth right because he knew and appreciated the value of it.

In the end, Jacob received the blessings instead of Esau even though he had to scheme with his mother's help to receive it. Isaac, who was almost completely blind by this time wanted to pass the Abrahamic Covenant Blessings on before he died. Therefore, he called his first born Esau to make ready his favorite meal so that after eating it, he can bless Esau but Rebekah their mother remembered the prophecy that she received. Having seen Esau's ways, she helped prepare Jacob to receive it instead. We see Jacob receiving the blessings in **Genesis 27:26-29**:

> "And **his father Isaac said unto him, Come near now, and kiss me, my son.** 27 And he came near, and kissed him: and he smelled the smell of his raiment, and blessed him, **and said, See, the smell of my son is as the smell of a field which the LORD hath blessed:** 28 <u>**Therefore God give thee of the dew of heaven,**</u> **and the fatness of the earth, and plenty of corn and wine:**

29 **Let people serve thee, and nations bow down to thee: <u>be lord over thy brethren, and let thy mother's sons bow down to thee: cursed be every one that curseth thee, and blessed be he that blesseth thee</u>.**"

Jacob successfully received the Abrahamic Covenant Blessings that cannot be revoked or disannul by any man. He sought the blessing carefully and was willing to do whatever was required to get it. Even his father trembled greatly when he realized that Jacob was the one that he blessed instead of Esau but what Esau did not know was that he opened the door for the blessings to go to Jacob the day he handed over his birth right to Jacob.

The blessings were to go to the first born but Esau made Jacob the first born in place of himself! I say again that he cried for a blessing from his father Isaac but it was too late as we can see in **Genesis 27:33-37**:

"**And Isaac trembled very exceedingly, and said, Who?** <u>where is he that hath taken venison, and brought it me, and I have eaten of all before thou camest, and have blessed him</u>? **yea, and he shall be blessed.** *34* **And when Esau heard the words of his father, he cried with a great and exceeding bitter cry, and said unto his father, Bless me, even me also, O my father.**

35 And he said, <u>Thy brother came with subtilty, and hath taken away thy blessing</u>.

36 And he said, Is not he rightly named Jacob? for he hath supplanted me these two times: he took away my birthright; and, behold, now he hath taken away my blessing. **And he said, Hast thou not reserved a blessing for me?**

37 <u>And Isaac answered and said unto Esau,</u> **Behold, I have made him thy lord, and all his brethren have I given to him for servants;** and with corn and wine have I sustained him: and **what shall I do now unto thee, my son?**"

Unlike his brother Esau who was rebellious towards his parents, Jacob was obedient to his parents. He followed the instructions that he was given by his father and his mother not to marry any of the Canaanites women. He was told to go to Haran and choose a wife there and he went. He left on the journey placing his trust in the Lord to guide him as he went.

While on this journey, God met with him and encouraged him by showing him a dream with a ladder that reached far into heaven. Jacob was able to see how close God was to him and he vowed to serve Him and Him only if God will protect and keep him safe in his journey. God went with him to Haran and kept him safe on the way.

"And he lighted upon a certain place, and tarried there all night, because the sun was set; and he took of the stones of that place, and put them for his pillows, and lay down in that place to sleep. 12 And he dreamed, and behold a ladder set up on the earth, and the top of it reached to heaven: and behold the angels of God ascending and descending on it.

13 And, behold, the LORD stood above it, and said, **I am the LORD God of Abraham thy father, and the God of Isaac: the land whereon thou liest, to thee will I give it , and to thy seed; 14 And thy seed shall be as the dust of the earth, and thou shalt spread abroad to the west, and to the east, and to the north, and to the south: and in thee and in thy seed shall all the families of the earth be blessed.**

15 **And, behold, I am with thee, and will keep thee in all places whither thou goest, and will bring thee again into this land; for I will not leave thee, until I have done that which I have spoken to thee of.** 16 And Jacob awaked out of his sleep, and he said, **Surely the LORD is in this place; and I knew it not"** (Genesis 28:11-16).

Understanding God's Infinite Wisdom and Knowledge

Looking back, the scriptures about God loving Jacob and hating Esau might seem unfair until you take into account God's infinite wisdom and knowledge. In the light of this wisdom and knowledge, we can truly appreciate how God was carefully behind the scene in making sure that His plans do not fall into the wrong hands and with this realization, the scriptures that initially seemed unfair to us such as, "Esau I hate, Jacob I love," begin to give us a different understanding from God's perspective.

Again, you can be rest assured in the knowledge that God is not partial nor is He a respecter of persons. What He did was to watch over His great blessing that was to be passed on and He made sure that the right person received it. He gave it to Jacob just as it was prophesied to Rebekah that the older shall serve the younger. As I said in the previous chapter, this is one of the reasons why Rebekah helped Jacob to receive the blessings. She was not a wicked schemer but was acting on the Word of the Lord that came to her.

This is why we must make the effort to know God and to know His ways because He sees what we cannot see and so when He acts, He makes sure that His desired ending is what will be accomplished. This can sometimes conflict with our finite mind and our sense of right and wrong because we cannot see what He sees and we do not know what He knows. Therefore, when we read scriptures, we have to take into consideration the knowledge and wisdom of God concerning His decisions because He alone is All-Knowing and He can see you even in your mother's womb. He already knows exactly how you are going to turn out in life.

Again, what God needed was someone that was not going to be rebellious but that would be tenderhearted towards Him and His kingdom and that would value the Abrahamic Covenant Blessings. Throughout the generations from Abraham, this became God's criteria for choosing who receives the blessing. For instance, before addressing why Judah received the Abrahamic Covenant Blessings, we are going to first take a look at why Levi ended up with the lineage of the priesthood among his brethren. It will clarify for you how God chooses. As soon as we finish taking a look at Levi, we will then address why Judah was chosen.

Chapter 4
Why Did God Choose Levi for the Priesthood?

Origin of the Levitical Priesthood

It is very interesting when you see how God went about choosing Levi; it reveals how that God is a master strategist. Yes, God is a master planner and He does actually supervise what goes on in human affairs. The Messiah is going to be a Priest; a High Priest. Therefore, God had to teach the children of Israel about the order of the priesthood. He chose the **Tribe of Levi for the Priesthood** and He chose the **Tribe of Judah as the tribe from which the Messiah would come**. Why did God give the covenant of the priesthood to Levi?

Levi's Zeal for God

Levi is one of the sons of Jacob and He is the grandfather of Moses, Aaron and all the descendents from which you have the Levitical priesthood. **They did not get it just because God woke up one morning and said Levi is going to be my priest. They earned it.** Let us look at **Malachi 2:4-8**, for how they earned it:

> "And ye shall know that I have sent this commandment unto you, **that my covenant might be with Levi**, saith the LORD of hosts. 5 My covenant was with him of life and peace; and I gave them to him **for the fear**

**wherewith he feared me, and was
afraid before my name.**

**6 The law of truth was in his mouth,
and iniquity was not found in his lips:
he walked with me in peace and equity,
and did turn many away from iniquity.**
7 For the priest's lips should keep
knowledge, and they should seek the
law at his mouth: for he is the messenger
of the LORD of hosts.

8 But ye are departed out of the way; ye
have caused many to stumble at the law;
ye have corrupted the covenant of Levi,
saith the LORD of hosts."

What is God talking about here? God is referring
to an event in which "Levi" (actually Levi's great
grandson, **Phinehas**) stood up for Him to enforce
His righteous requirement in the days of Moses.
Numbers 25:6-13 explains in detail what happened
and how Phinehas stood up for God. We will
look at this historical account of the events in the
very next sub-chapter because it shows how God
rewarded Phinehas for standing up to enforce
God's commandment in the midst of all of the
children of Israel.

When God initially commanded Moses to
anoint Aaron and his sons to be priests unto
Him, He did not make it a perpetual order of
priesthood. It was in the days of **Phinehas**
that God established the Levitical order of
priesthood forever.

The Valiant Act of Phinehas -Levi's Great Grandson

Again, the event that God referred to in **Malachi 2:4-8** took place in the wilderness during the days of Moses. When God brought the children of Israel out of Egypt and into the wilderness; He told them that He did not want them to marry any of the daughters of the people of the land that they are going to possess because He did not want the people of those lands to teach them idolatry. Therefore, it was a great sin in those days for any son of the Israelites to marry a Midianite, a Canaanite, an Amalakite or any other foreign women in any of the lands that they came to possess. **After many years, they became rebellious and many of them took to themselves Midianite wives.**

God was very angry with them that He sent a plague into the camp because many of them had married Midianite women. As a result of the plague that God sent into the camp of Israel, many people in the camp began to die. When Moses went to find out from the Lord why there was a plague in the camp and people were dying, God told him that it was because many of them had gone and joined themselves to Baalpeor (Baal) through their marriages or unions with Midianite women.

The entire congregation along with Moses came together and began to pray and to repent of the sin of marrying strange wives. While they were doing this, a certain man of Israel walked into the camp with his Midianite wife in the middle of this repentance session. No one said anything to the man or the woman but one of Levi's great-grandson (Aaron's grandson) named **Phinehas.** Phinehas could not stand the defilement and he took the necessary action by killing both the man and his Midianite wife. **Phinehas had a zeal for the Lord and a zeal for righteousness. He boldly and fearlessly enforced God's judgment in the presence of all the children of Israel.**

This event took place in **Numbers 25:6-13 and it reveals to us why the Levites (Phinehas' tribe) received the Levitical priesthood. They received "covenant of an everlasting priesthood" because of Phinehas' valiant action:**

> "And, behold, one of the children of Israel came and brought unto his brethren a Midianitish woman in the sight of Moses, and in the sight of all the congregation of the children of Israel, who were weeping before the door of the tabernacle of the congregation *(because of the sin of being joined to baalpeor).*

> 7 **And when Phinehas, the son of Eleazar, the son of Aaron the priest, saw it, he rose up from among the congregation, and took a javelin in his hand;** 8 **And he went after the man of Israel into the tent, and thrust both of them through, the man of Israel, and the woman through her belly.** So the plague was stayed from the children of Israel.

9 And those that died in the plague were twenty and four thousand. *10* And the LORD spake unto Moses, saying, *11* Phinehas, the son of Eleazar, the son of Aaron the priest, hath turned my wrath away from the children of Israel, while he was zealous for my sake among them, that I consumed not the children of Israel in my jealousy.

12 Wherefore say, Behold, I give unto him my covenant of peace: *13* And he shall have it, and his seed after him, even the covenant of an everlasting priesthood; because he was zealous for his God, and made an atonement for the children of Israel."

As you can see, the fact that Levi became the lineage of the "everlasting priesthood" was not by accident. It was a reward for what Phinehas, the great grandson of Levi did. I wanted you to see how Levi got the "everlasting priesthood" because it proves my point that God is not a respecter of persons. As I said, He merely rewards whoever deserves it. As we saw in scriptures, the Levites were not able to keep the priesthood forever but God in His wisdom had a backup plan. This plan involved His only begotten son, Jesus.

A Future Priesthood after the Order of Melchisedec

Although God made the tribe of Levi the lineage

of the Priesthood forever, they were only able to keep it up to the time of Eli; the High Priest in the days of the Prophet Samuel. Since the time of Moses, <u>the tribe of Levi had the Priesthood but they became corrupt and under Eli and his sons who were the last priest from the house of Aaron,</u> God abolished the priesthood.

<u>They did not keep the terms of the covenant that God made with them concerning the priesthood therefore, God stripped the Priesthood from them. The Prophet Samuel took over and Israel began to have Judges in place of High Priests</u> **but God had another Priesthood prepared in His Son Jesus — a Priesthood that is rooted in the power of an Everlasting or Endless Life.**

When you read **1 Samuel 3:11-14**, you will see details of how the Levites did not obey the terms of the covenant that God made with them, and how God judged the house of Eli; the last Levite priest and how He abolished the priesthood.

"And the LORD said to Samuel, <u>Behold, I will do a thing in Israel, at which</u> <u>both the ears of every one that heareth it shall tingle.</u> 12 <u>In that day I will perform against Eli all things which I have spoken concerning his house: when I begin, I will also make an end.</u>

13 **For I have told him that I will judge his house forever** <u>**for the iniquity which he knoweth;**</u> **because his sons** *(the last two priests)* **made themselves**

vile, and he restrained them not.
14 And therefore I have sworn unto
the house of Eli, that **the iniquity of
Eli's house shall not be purged with
sacrifice nor offering** forever."

God brought about this judgment against Eli and his
sons on the day that the Ark of the Covenant was
captured. Both Eli, his sons and even his grandson
that was born on this same day of the battle all died.
Thus, the High Priest Eli died leaving behind no heir.
Therefore, Samuel the Prophet became the Judge in
Israel. Without any high priest, Israel came under
the rule of judges and after the judges, then under
the rule of Kings.

The Kings then began to appoint their own
High Priests as well as the rest of the priesthood
positions but as I stated before, God in His wisdom
had provided a different type of priesthood that was
going to come about in Christ. We see this recorded
in **Hebrews 7:14-17**:

"**For it is evident that our Lord sprang
out of Juda; of which tribe Moses
spake nothing concerning priesthood.**
15 And it is yet far more evident: for
that after the similitude of Melchisedec
there ariseth another priest, 16 **Who
is made, not after the law of a carnal
commandment, but after the power
of an endless life.** 17 **For he testifieth,
Thou art a priest for ever after the
order of Melchisedec** *(i.e., after the order
of everlasting life).*"

Not knowing this backup plan that God made in His Son, the Jewish leaders in the days of Jesus looked at him and said He is not a Levite; how can he be a priest? They rejected Jesus because He was not a Levite. They did this because they had no clue that God in His infinite wisdom knew that the Levites were not going to be able to keep the terms of the covenant that He made with them so He made a secondary provision in which He would begin another type of priesthood that is based on the power of an everlasting or an endless life.

God waited for thousands of years to see His plan for a different priesthood come to pass in Christ. This is why I said that the way that Levi was chosen and what happened afterwards are very good insights into how God presides over human affairs to make sure that His plans and His purposes on earth are accomplished just the way He wants them.

We have seen how and why God chose Levi and gave him the covenant of the priesthood but remember that Jacob gave the rulership or the Scepter to Judah as part of his blessings upon Judah. What we are looking for is why Judah received this particular blessing instead of his brothers? What did he do differently from his brothers?

Chapter 5
Determining the Tribe of the Messiah

Why Was Judah Chosen?

After seeing why Levi was chosen as the tribe or lineage of the Priesthood, let us now see why Judah was chosen as the tribe or lineage of the Messiah. I have already established the fact that God does not chose people arbitrary, but He rewards well doing and He chooses for a purpose and with a purpose. Therefore, the question that you should be asking now is, why was Judah chosen to rule over his brethren? **Micah 5:2** tells us that the **Messiah would come from Bethlehem, Judah**:

> **"But thou, <u>Bethlehem Ephratah</u>, though thou be little among the thousands of <u>Judah</u>, yet out of thee shall <u>he</u> come forth unto me that is to be ruler in Israel; <u>whose goings forth have been from of old, from everlasting</u>** *(the Messiah)*.**"**

This is talking about the Messiah; therefore it is telling us that the Lord is going to come from Bethlehem, Judah and He did! The Lord Jesus was born to the house of David, in the city of Bethlehem and in the tribe of Judah and what you see in this is that God is no respecter of persons but He rewards well doing. In other words, God does not go "eeny, meeny, miny, moe" when trying to determine who to choose, but He picks those who do well and He rewards or blesses them.

Let us take a second look at the fact that while releasing the covenant blessing unto his 12 sons,

Jacob was under the anointing and he chose Judah as the ruler over his brethren and as the lineage of the Messiah according to **Genesis 49:10:**

> **"The Scepter** *(ruler-ship)* **shall not depart from Judah, nor a lawgiver from between his feet, <u>until Shiloh</u> <u>come</u>** *(Shiloh is the prophetic name of the Messiah and it means the Prince of Peace);* **and unto him shall the gathering of the people be."**

It says that there will not cease to be a lawgiver in Judah until the coming of the Shiloh and the Jews knew that the coming of Shiloh referred to the coming of the Messiah. We know that Jacob loved Joseph more than all His other children and after Joseph, he loved Benjamin. Left to Jacob, he would have given the rulership to either Joseph or to Benjamin his two favorite children but he did not do that.

The question is, why then did Jacob give the rulership to Judah? The answer is because it was God's decision to reward Judah for what Judah had done. Therefore, it was the Holy Spirit that moved through Jacob as he spoke the blessings. It is just like the case of Noah who was drunk when one of his sons looked upon his nakedness and when it came time for him to also speak blessings upon his children under the anointing, he blessed his other sons but judged the son that had looked upon his nakedness and "blabbed" about it to his brothers. Under the anointing, Noah made that son a servant to his two other brothers! He actually judged the entire lineage of the son that saw his nakedness and talked about it.

You can read about this event for yourself in **Genesis 9:20-27**. It is the same way that by the anointing, Jacob knew that Reuben his first son had slept with one of his concubines and he judged Reuben for it also. **Before we examine what Judah did to earn the reward of the lineage of the Messiah, let us first look at how God introduced the ransom principle to the earth realm because it ties directly to what Judah did.**

God Introduces the Ransom Principle

What is interesting about Noah and Jacob concerning their situations is that both Noah and Jacob were being supervised by God to make sure that His plan was carried out according to His desired principles. God was trying to make sure that the principle that He had put in place with Abraham and even from the Garden of Eden was carried out according to His plan and purpose.

In other words, after Adam and Eve sinned in the Garden of Eden, God slew an innocent lamb and He used the skin and the blood of the lamb to cover both Adam and Eve. By doing this, God set up a principle of redemption; **holding the innocent responsible for the sin of the guilty. This principle spoke to the coming of Christ as God's lamb to be slain for the sin of the world**. He continued this principle with Abraham by requiring the sacrifice of Isaac and it is called—**the principle of substitution or the ransom principle.**

What this means is that God substituted His innocent Son Jesus for guilty humanity. As a result, the Lord Jesus paid for the sin that all humanity has committed against God. Sacrificing the Lord Jesus on the Cross is the ransom that God paid for our sins against Him. **A ransom is defined as "the price or payment demanded" for the release of a person or property.**

In this case, the Lord Jesus is the ransom price for the release of all humanity from the original sin *(rebellion)* against God. **The ransom was paid to God by Jesus because God's judgment that "the soul that sinneth shall die"** *(Ezekiel 18:20)* **had to be satisfied but there was not an innocent man or woman on earth because we had all sinned against God.** We should all be grateful that God introduced the ransom principle on earth because it paved the way for the coming of the Lord Jesus.

How the Ransom Principle Works
We saw that after Adam and Eve sinned, God sacrificed a lamb and covered them both with the blood and the skin of the lamb. We also saw how that the lamb was **a type of Christ.** This is way when we became born again, we are covered with the blood of Jesus and the Bible says that **if you are baptized into Christ, you have put on Christ** just like Adam and Eve put on the blood and the skin of the lamb that God slew in the Garden of Eden to cover them:

"**For as many of you as have been baptized into Christ have put on Christ**" (Galatians 3:27).

52

God did the work of redemption in the realm of the spirit in the garden but He needed a man on earth so that the work can be manifested in the earth realm physically. As a result, God went on a man-hunt and He found the man Abraham!

We saw earlier that God made Abraham to wait until he was 100 years old before he gave him a son and God made sure that this son was really and truly precious to Abraham. Again, Abraham was 100 years old and Sarah was 90 years old so that the birth of this son was a miracle in itself. As a result, Isaac was much beloved by his father and mother but just when they thought that they could really enjoy this child, God requested that Abraham take the child up to Mount Moriah and slay him as a sacrifice to Him.

Abraham Willing Offered Up Isaac to God
In obedience to the instruction from God, Abraham took Isaac as commanded and went up to Mount Moriah to sacrifice him there. He built an altar and laid his much beloved son on it and took a knife to slay him and when God saw that Abraham willingly gave up his son, God stopped him and gave Abraham a lamb to sacrifice instead. **This is the type of man that God is looking for even today; a man that loves Him and will not withhold anything from Him**.

God's Response to Abraham
Hebrews 11:17-19 tells us what God did in response to Abraham's willingness to offer up his beloved Isaac. **When Abraham willingly offered**

up his much beloved son Isaac, God also without reservation offered up His only begotten Son Jesus Christ to pay the ransom price for our sins.

> "By faith Abraham, when he was tried, offered up Isaac: **and <u>he that had received the promises</u>** *(God)* **offered up his only begotten son** *(Jesus),* **18** Of whom it was said, **That in Isaac shall thy seed be called:** *19* Accounting that God was able to raise him up, even from the dead; from whence also he received him in a figure."

In other words, God made the Lord Jesus the ransom lamb to be sacrificed for the sin of the world. **The ransom is the scapegoat that takes the blame for those who are guilty while the guilty go free!** We all deserved to die and go to hell for all the sins or wickedness that we have committed but instead, God decided to have mercy on us and have His only begotten son; the Lord Jesus take the blame for us on the Cross.

The Lord Jesus became guilty of all our sins. He traded place with us on the Cross and became the substitute or scapegoat that God held responsible for all our sins. On the Cross, He died a very agonizing, slow and painful death and He was put to shame publicly. **They made a public spectacle of Him, laughed and scorned Him while He was on the Cross <u>but He overlooked all of it and made intercession to the Father to forgive us because we had no idea of what we were doing.</u>** As a result of His intercession for us on the Cross, **today and for all of eternity, His**

blood cries forgiveness to the Father on our behalf as opposed to the blood of righteous Abel that cries to God for vengeance!

Therefore, you can safely say that God found in Abraham a man after His own heart that will do all His will when Abraham did not withhold his son from God. He was willing to obey God's instructions even when the instructions required that he kill his much beloved son, Isaac. **I will like to reiterate that the Lord Jesus' obedience to His Father's command to go to the Cross is the highest obedience. Obedience does not get any better than this.** Your love for God will make you obey Him. The Lord said it Himself in **John 15:13** that:

> "Greater love hath no man than this, that a man lay down his life for his friends."

As you can see, the Lord Jesus came into the world as a ransom lamb to be sacrificed (as a type of Isaac to be slain). **First, we see Him in the Garden of Eden as the slain lamb, and again we see Him in Isaac as a type of a lamb to be slain in what God was doing through Abraham concerning Isaac. Finally, He appeared physically in the earth as the Lamb of God and He was truly slain on the Cross for the sin of the world.**

The beauty in these events is that **by willingly offering up Isaac, Abraham provided God with the opportunity to successfully establish the ransom principle in the earth realm.** We have already seen how God chose Jacob as the seed from Isaac to be the next custodian of the Abrahamic Covenant Blessings. So, again, God goes on another man-hunt among the seeds of Jacob.

This now brings us to the 12 sons of Jacob who are now the 12 tribes of Israel; the grandsons of Isaac but only one of them as you will soon discover will actually tap into the ransom or the substitution principle. We are going to see how Judah is the only one of all the sons of Jacob who fulfilled the requirement for this ransom or substitution principle.

Chapter 6
How Did Judah Fulfill
the Ransom Principle?

Now we are going to look at the events that opened the door for **Judah** to tap into the ransom principle and thereby made him the only eligible son of Jacob to receive the Abrahamic Covenant Blessing of the Messiah's lineage. These events had to do with what happened between Jacob, the 12 brothers, and in particular what happened concerning Joseph and Benjamin.

About the Man Judah

Judah was not noted in the Bible as being particularly a better person than any of the other sons of Jacob while they were growing up. As I said before, it was Joseph that was recorded as being elevated by his father above his older brothers. Because Jacob made Joseph his favorite son, all of his brothers became jealous of him. They envied and resented him because he being one of the youngest, was being positioned by their father to rule over them. All his brothers hated him including Judah.

The Wickedness of Joseph's Brothers towards Him

To make matters worse, Joseph began to have dreams that confirmed his older brothers' fear that he would rule over them because his dreams showed all his brothers bowing down to him. Therefore, the brothers with the exception of Benjamin who was too young at the time and had the same mother as Joseph decided to make sure that Joseph's dreams did not come to pass.

We know the story of how they could not kill him but came up with the plan to sell him into slavery instead and they did. They all went home and lied to their father that Joseph was dead as recorded in **Genesis 37:18-28**:

> "And when they saw him afar off, even before he came near unto them, they conspired against him to slay him. *19* And they said one to another, **Behold, this dreamer cometh.** *20* **Come now therefore, and let us slay him, and cast him into some pit, and we will say, Some evil beast hath devoured him: and we shall see what will become of his dreams.**

> *21* And Reuben heard it, and he delivered him out of their hands; and said, Let us not kill him. *22* And Reuben said unto them, Shed no blood, but cast him into this pit that is in the wilderness, and lay no hand upon him; that he might rid him out of their hands, to deliver him to his father again. *23* And it came to pass, when Joseph was come unto his brethren, that they stripped Joseph out of his coat, his coat of many colors that was on him;

24 And they took him, and cast him into a pit: and the pit was empty, there was no water in it. 25 **And they sat down to eat bread**: and they lifted up their eyes and looked, and, behold, a company of Ishmaelites came from Gilead with their camels bearing spices and balm and myrrh, going to carry it down to Egypt. 26 **And Judah said unto his brethren, What profit is it if we slay our brother, and conceal his blood?**

27 **Come, and let us sell him to the Ishmaelites, and let not our hand be upon him; for he is our brother and our flesh.** And his brethren were content. 28 Then there passed by Midianites merchantmen; and they drew and lifted up Joseph out of the pit, and sold Joseph to the Ishmaelites for twenty pieces of silver: and they brought Joseph into Egypt."

Judah Was Part of the Conspirators against Joseph

As you can see, it was **Judah** who suggested that they sell Joseph into slavery. What we learn from this is that initially, Judah was not better than any of his other brothers. Yes, Judah was part of the conspiracy against Joseph because he resented Joseph as much as his other brothers did. All the brothers including Judah had no remorse over throwing Joseph into a pit but rather, they all sat down to enjoy their dinner after throwing Joseph into the pit. This is a serious wickedness and without remorse, they added to their wickedness by selling Joseph into slavery!

With Joseph sold, the brothers told Jacob their father that they believed that Joseph had been killed by a wild beast because they found his bloody coat in the wilderness. Their father believed their report that Joseph was dead and he mourned for his son for many years. These sons of Jacob hated Joseph so much that they would rather watch their father pine away in sorrow over Joseph for more than 10 years than tell him the truth that Joseph was alive!

Many years after the Joseph incident, it looks like **Judah** became a better person because we going to see him act differently with a better heart. As we will see later, it looks like he wanted to now do the right thing from the way that he spoke to both his father Jacob and to Joseph.

Meanwhile, Joseph went down into Egypt as a slave and suffered for 13 years as a slave but later became the Prime Minister of Egypt. Joseph's circumstances changed when he successfully interpreted the Pharaoh's dream and he also helped to devise a plan to save Egypt from an impending famine. As a result of his position in Egypt, it was Joseph who determined who can buy food in Egypt when the years of famine came as he had predicted. In due time, the famine spread to Canaan where Jacob and his family dwelt.

Jacob sent 10 of his now 11 sons to Egypt to buy

corn there because there was no corn in Canaan and Joseph immediately recognized them as soon as he saw them in Egypt. He began to deal roughly with them as he accused them of being spies and they had to prove to Joseph that they were not spies. By the time they were ready to go, Joseph held Simeon as his hostage until the brothers can prove that they were not spies by bringing their youngest brother Benjamin as a proof that they were indeed 11 brothers from the same father.

Why Joseph Detained Simeon

Why did Joseph choose Simeon as his hostage? The answer is because Simeon was the trouble maker and the ring leader among the brothers. He was the one that came up with the plan along with Levi his younger brother to kill the entire city of the Hivites when Shechem the Son of King Hamor; prince of Hivite slept with Jacob's daughter Dinah.

The prince offered to marry her afterwards and Jacob agreed. As a result, Jacob made a deal with King Hamor to offer his daughter Dinah in marriage to the king's son if the King and his household would become circumcised. The king honored the deal that he made with Jacob and required that every male in his city become circumcised and they all did including himself and his household.

Simeon, knowing that all the Hivite males were very sore from their circumcision, devised a plan with Levi his brother (another son of Leah) to go and kill off all the males because he knew that they will not be able to fight because of their circumcision wounds and they did; killing all the males in the city.

> "And it came to pass on the third day, when they were sore, that two of the sons of Jacob, <u>Simeon and Levi, Dinah's</u> <u>brethren, took each man his</u> <u>sword, and came upon the city boldly,</u> <u>and slew all the males.</u> 26 And they slew Hamor and Shechem his son with the edge of the sword, and took Dinah out of Shechem's house, and went out" (Genesis 34:25-26).

They totally disregarded the agreement that Jacob their father made with the King and his son, Shechem by taking matters into their own hands. **This is why Jacob said that Simeon and Levi have the "instruments of cruelty" in their habitation when it came time for him to speak a blessing over them.** Jacob could not bless them but instead denounced them. Below is what Jacob said about them:

> "<u>Simeon and Levi are brethren;</u> instruments of cruelty are in their habitations. 6 <u>O my soul, come not thou</u> <u>into their secret; unto their assembly,</u> <u>mine honour, be not thou united:</u> for in their anger they slew a man, and in their selfwill they digged down a wall. 7 Cursed be their anger, for it was fierce; and their wrath, for it was cruel: I will divide them in Jacob, and scatter them in Israel" (Genesis 49:5-7).

You can see therefore that by holding back Simeon (who is older than Levi) as a hostage, Joseph's intention was to make sure that the Simeon the ringleader was not going to brew a new plan to counteract what Joseph was trying to accomplish by the way that he was dealing with all his brothers. Meaning that with Simeon detained by Joseph, the rest of the brothers might have a little peace on the way home because he will not be there to inspire them to plan some wickedness.

Jacob's Refusal to Send Benjamin to Egypt

The brothers got back home and they told Jacob their father that the man in Egypt (Joseph) was very rough with them and that he had detained Simeon and will not release him until they can prove that they are not spies by bringing their youngest brother Benjamin with them the next time that they come to Egypt. Jacob said no to the request to send Benjamin to Egypt.

Months went by and Jacob was still completely against sending off Benjamin to Egypt because he did not want to lose Benjamin as he lost Joseph. They were his only children from his very beloved Rachel. This standoff with their father continued until they completely ran out of the corn that they bought in Egypt and they now needed to go again to get more corn.

A Golden Opportunity for God to Find His Man

From God's perspective, this is a golden opportunity to see if any of the sons of Jacob will become the man He is looking for to be the next custodian of the Abrahamic Covenant Blessings. Another way to say this is that Jacob and his sons have a problem but to God, this is an opportunity to see who is going to be His man among these 12 brothers. **Remember that initially, God was looking for a man on earth and He found Abraham. Next, He chose Isaac and after that He chose Jacob but now, He needs to choose from Jacob's sons.**

God wants a man that He is going to release the blessings to but He does not just give it to anyone even if they are all Jacob's sons. **To God, receiving the blessings has to be earned through a righteous act. Even today, only those who believe in Christ receive the blessing of salvation. It is not given to everyone on earth but to those who demonstrate their faith in the finished works of Christ. God counts our faith as righteousness just as Abraham's faith was counted as righteousness. Therefore, from God's perspective, the plea from Jacob's sons with their father to release Benjamin to go with them to Egypt became the litmus test to see who will be God's man.** In other words, who among them is willing to be the scapegoat or the ransom for Benjamin?

Reuben's Plea to Jacob to Release Benjamin to Him

The first brother to make a plea was Reuben but **he was not willing to endanger himself or volunteer himself as the scapegoat** should anything happen to Benjamin in their journey. Look at his response to the situation in **Genesis 42:36-37:**

> "And Jacob their father said unto them,
> Me have ye bereaved of my children:
> Joseph is not, and Simeon is not, and ye
> will take Benjamin away: all these things
> are against me. 37 **And Reuben spake
> unto his father, saying, <u>Slay my two
> sons</u>, if I bring him not to thee: deliver
> him into my hand, and I will bring him
> to thee again.**"

Reuben is not bargaining with himself but with his two sons so Jacob refused to release Benjamin to go with them to Egypt. Again, as you can clearly see from Reuben's plea, he is not willing to put himself in harm's way but he would rather endanger the lives of his children. Therefore, Jacob does not accept his plea.

Judah's Plea to Jacob to Release Benjamin to Him

None of the other brothers spoke up after Reuben but Judah. In **Genesis 43:8-9,** we see Judah's plea to Jacob his father:

> "And **Judah said unto Israel his father**,
> <u>Send the lad with me, and we will arise
> and go; that we may live, and not die,
> both we, and thou, and also our little
> ones.</u> 9 **I will be surety** *(scapegoat)* **for
> him; of my hand shalt thou require
> him: if I bring him not unto thee, and
> set him before thee, then <u>let me bear
> the blame for ever</u>.**"

You can clearly see how Judah made it personal with

his father by telling his father to hold him personally responsible if any harm ever befell Benjamin in their journey to Egypt. **In other words, Judah told his father to make him the scapegoat if he does not come back with Benjamin. Thus, Judah without knowing what was at stake took the first step into the ransom principle by his willingness to put himself on the line for Benjamin his brother!** This promise by Judah to be the scapegoat will be tested later.

Based on Judah's plea, Jacob released Benjamin to go with his brothers into Egypt and when they got to Egypt, Joseph released Simeon to them because they had brought Benjamin with them. **You need to remember that the brothers are still being tested by Joseph and God will give Judah an opportunity to make good on his promise to become the ransom or the scapegoat should any harm come to Benjamin.**

Joseph's Plan With His Wine Cup
The brothers enjoyed a brief period of merriment with Joseph as they dined with him and Joseph's heart was moved towards his younger brother Benjamin and he now wants to keep Benjamin with him in Egypt. Therefore, he devised a plan to plant his favorite wine cup in Benjamin's sack so that he can use the accusation of being a thief as an excuse to detain Benjamin and thereby have Benjamin with him in Egypt for good.

Joseph's plan ran into a snag because **Judah had become surety for the boy to Jacob their father.**

Therefore, when they discovered the wine cup in Benjamin's sack and Joseph proceeded to make Benjamin "his slave forever," Judah would not have it. He now has to make good on his promise to be held responsible should anything bad happen to Benjamin his brother.

Judah Stepped Forward as the Ransom for Benjamin

Judah sprang up and looked Joseph squarely in the face as he said NO to Benjamin being Joseph's "slave forever." **Instead, he offered himself up in place of Benjamin to be Joseph's "slave forever"—to be the scapegoat!** What this means is that Judah stepped up and told Joseph to take him as his "slave forever" in place of Benjamin and that Joseph should allow Benjamin to go home to their father. Remember that the definition of a ransom is **"the price or payment demanded for the release of a person or property." Thus, Judah tapped into the ransom principle!**

Yes, Judah made good on his promise to be surety for Benjamin and in so doing became a type of ransom or a scapegoat for Benjamin his brother. This selfless act earned him the reward of being the tribe through which God's ultimate ransom or scapegoat; the Lord Jesus would come. Let us look at Judah's ransom plea to Joseph in **Genesis 44:23-34:**

> "And thou saidst unto thy servants, Except your youngest brother come down with you, ye shall see my face no

more. 24 And it came to pass when we came up unto thy servant my father, we told him the words of my lord. 25 And our father said, Go again, and buy us a little food.

26 And we said, We cannot go down: if our youngest brother be with us, then will we go down: for we may not see the man's face, except our youngest brother be with us.

27 And thy servant my father said unto us, Ye know that my wife bare me two sons: 28 And the one went out from me, and I said, Surely he is torn in pieces; and I saw him not since: 29 And if ye take this also from me, and mischief befall him, ye shall bring down my gray hairs with sorrow to the grave (*Now, Judah begins to plead with Joseph*).

30 Now therefore when I come to thy servant my father, and the lad be not with us; seeing that his life is bound up in the lad's life; 31 It shall come to pass, when he seeth that the lad is not with us, that he will die: and thy servants shall bring down the gray hairs of thy servant our father with sorrow to the grave.

32 **For thy servant became surety** (*scapegoat*) **for the lad unto my father, saying, If I bring him not unto thee,**

then I shall bear the blame to my father forever. 33 **Now therefore, I pray thee, let thy servant** *(meaning himself)* **abide instead of the lad a bondman to my lord; and let the lad go up with his brethren.**

34 For how shall I go up to my father, and the lad be not with me? lest peradventure I see the evil that shall come on my father."

Again, can you see that of all the sons of Jacob, it was only Judah that tapped into the ransom principle and thereby positioned himself to receive the lineage of the Messiah because the Messiah Himself is coming as a ransom!

What I wanted you to see by taking you through the chronology of these events is that Judah did not just get that lineage of the Messiah from nowhere. Because as I have stated over and over again, God does not play favorites but He rewards whoever does well. All of the children of Jacob were well positioned to receive the Abrahamic Covenant Blessings but they all had to meet the requirement for receiving the blessings and only Judah met that requirement.

As you can see, it was given to Judah as a reward because he was the only one among the brothers who would substitute himself and put himself in harm's way for his brother Benjamin. For this, he earned the right to become the person and through whose tribe the true ransom (the Messiah) was going to come.

The significance of what Judah did became apparent when Jacob began to speak the Abrahamic Covenant Blessings under the anointing. The Holy Spirit led him to release the blessings of the Messianic Lineage unto Judah who was already positioned by his actions to receive it. Thus, Judah received the blessings from God through his father Jacob and his tribe has now become the tribe through which the Messiah will come.

What we learn from this is that first, God positions a person for a blessing and then He releases the blessing to the person. In line with this positioning of the right person who deserves the reward, He then revealed to me why it was that Jacob was able to successfully receive the Abrahamic Covenant Blessings instead of his brother Esau. According to Him, Jacob was able to scheme successfully with his mother's help to receive the blessings instead of his brother Esau because Esau had already positioned Jacob to receive the blessings by giving away his birthright to him!

By doing this, Esau made a covenant with Jacob that Jacob will inherit all the benefits of the first born and Jacob did. God is a God of Covenant and He watches over all the covenants that we make. For a detailed teaching on Covenants, see my book that is titled: *"Understanding the Power of Covenants."*

I will like to state again that God does not play "eeny, meeny, miny, moe" when making a choice concerning us, instead, He waits until a person comes along that fulfills the requirement that He needs and He releases the blessing to the person. He loved all of Jacob's sons but each one of them had the same opportunity as Judah to step up into righteousness and become eligible to receive the blessing. This is one of the aspects of God's nature that most people are not familiar with—God's longsuffering. He can wait for hundreds of years for a person to meet His requirements before His particular purpose is manifested on earth.

Now God Needs a Man from the Tribe of Judah

We have seen how God chose Abraham and how since Abraham He has carefully guided and supervised how the blessing is passed on from one generation to another amongst the descendants of Abraham. **He has released the blessing to Judah so that Judah has become the lineage from which the Messiah would come.**

Now, God needs a man from the tribe of Judah that will carry the Abrahamic Covenant Blessings forward. In other words, He needs to find the next custodian of the blessings within the tribe of Judah but in the time being, several generations have gone by since the days of Judah. It has actually been more than 11 generations since the days of Judah but during the days of the Prophet Samuel, the children of Israel asked God for a king and God gave them Saul to be their first King.

Well, King Saul was not one to obey God's instructions because he liked to interpret God's instruction according to his own desire or will. Therefore, God was not pleased with him and He rejected him as king over Israel. For example, God gave King Saul the instruction to invade Amalek and to kill the Amalekites and not spare even the animals but to destroy everyone and everything in Amalek. Saul thought about the instruction and decided that it was not good to kill off all the animals so he kept most of them. He also kept alive the king of Amalek that God also told him to destroy.

God informed the Prophet Samuel about what King Saul had done and Samuel was furious as he confronted King Saul about his disobedience to God's instruction. **King Saul did not see anything wrong with what he had done as he told Samuel that they kept the animals so that they could sacrifice them to God.** We read about this in **1 Samuel 15:20-23**:

> "And Saul said unto Samuel, <u>Yea, I</u> have <u>obeyed the voice of the LORD,</u> <u>and have</u> <u>gone the way which the LORD sent</u> <u>me, and have brought Agag</u> <u>the king of</u> <u>Amalek, and have utterly</u> <u>destroyed the</u> <u>Amalekites.</u> 21 <u>But the</u> <u>people took of the</u> <u>spoil, sheep and oxen,</u> <u>the chief of the</u> <u>things which should</u> <u>have been utterly</u> <u>destroyed, to sacrifice</u> <u>unto the LORD</u> <u>thy God in Gilgal.</u>
>
> 22 And Samuel said, **Hath the LORD as great delight in burnt offerings and**

sacrifices, as in obeying the voice of the LORD? Behold, to obey is better than sacrifice, and to hearken than the fat of rams. 23 For rebellion is as the sin of witchcraft, and stubbornness is as iniquity and idolatry. <u>Because thou hast rejected the word of the LORD, he hath also rejected thee from being king.</u>"

The Prophet Samuel was so angry with King Saul for his disobedience to God's instruction that he stripped the kingdom away from Saul. The Prophet Samuel himself had to execute God's instruction by personally killing the King of Amalek and the animals that King Saul had spared.

From God's perspective, although King Saul was still sitting on the throne of Israel; spiritually, Israel was without a king. This became an interesting situation because God has been looking for a man within the tribe of Judah. Therefore, this became a perfect opportunity for God to locate His man within the tribe of Judah.

Again, God goes on a man-hunt within the tribe of Judah. His search brought Him to the house of Jesse.

Chapter 7
Why God Chose David and His Promises to David

King Saul's Disobedience is a Golden Opportunity

When King Saul disobeyed God's instruction, **the Prophet Samuel went into fasting for days while dressed in sack clothes but as I said earlier, God went on a man hunt within the Tribe of Judah and He found that man in the house of Jesse and in the person of young David.** Why did He choose David? Remember what I have been saying throughout this book that God is not an "arbitrary chooser" but a rewarder of those that do well according to His Word?

God actually combed the tribe of Judah until He saw young David. It is interesting to note that while God was at Jesse's house, He examined all of Jesse's children but only David met God's requirements. What this means is that God actually tried the hearts of all of Jesse's children and rejected all of them except for young David! He saw David's genuine love for Him, his daily devotion to Him, his devotion to His Word as well David's love for the nation of Israel.

David's Demonstration of His Love for God

What is amazing is that although he was very young, David was not ashamed to publicly express his love for God in his love letters to God. Yes, David wrote love letters in the form of Psalms to God continually. David was having a love affair with God while tending the sheep in the wilderness. In his love letters, David lets God know that His trust is in Him and that he knows that God cannot fail him.

He extolled and exalted God above all things in life and played the harp for God's enjoyment. He danced before God and learned to be totally dependent on God to help him fight off any adversary such as the lion and the bear. He had a very bold faith in God's abilities and faithfulness. **God responded by personally coming to his house to choose him as King and to position him to receive the Abrahamic Covenant Blessings**.

The following is David's account of his selection by God to rule Israel in **1 Chronicles 28:4**:

> "**Howbeit the LORD God of Israel chose me before all the house of my father to be king over Israel forever:** for he hath chosen Judah to be the ruler; **and of the house of Judah, the house of my father; and among the sons of my father he liked me to make me king over all Israel**."

God Sends the Prophet Samuel to Jesse's House

Again, just like the children of Jacob, all of Jesse's children had an equal opportunity to do well and to be selected by God for the lineage of the Messiah but just like Judah, only David

met God's requirement. Thus, God found Himself a man in the house of Jesse and in the person of young David.

Meanwhile, the Prophet Samuel was still praying and fasting for the nation that is now spiritually left without a king. He was very distraught about what happened with King Saul but while he was still mourning over Saul, God said the following to him in **1 Samuel 16:1**:

> "And the LORD said unto Samuel, **How long wilt thou mourn for Saul, seeing I have rejected him** from reigning over Israel? fill thine horn with oil, and go, I <u>will send thee to Jesse the Bethlehemite</u> *(of the tribe of Judah)*: **for I have provided me a king among his sons**."

In other words, God told the Prophet Samuel to stop mourning and get up from the place of sadness and go anoint the new king that He found in the house of Jesse! I will reiterate again that when God got to the house of Jesse, He tried every one of Jesse's sons before choosing David. The Prophet Samuel's only problem was that he did not know which one of Jesse's sons God had chosen. I think David was the eighth son and the last child of Jesse. He was not in the house when the Prophet Samuel came in and his father did not even invite him to the meeting with Samuel. As a result, young David had no clue as to what was going on in his father's house.

God Rejects David's Brothers and Chooses David

Samuel looked at Jesse's first son Eliab and he saw that Eliab was huge and well built just like King Saul, so Samuel thought; this must be God's man. He remembered that King Saul was chosen because of his stature; he was head and shoulder taller than anyone else. In other words, to Samuel, Eliab had the physical quality of a king; taller than everybody, huge, and he looked like one who can lead the people to victory in a war. He had a commanding built but to Samuel's amazement, God said not to anoint him because He had **rejected him.** We see this in **1 Samuel 16:7-13:**

> "But the LORD said unto Samuel, **Look not on his countenance, or on the height of his stature; because I have refused him: for the LORD seeth not as man seeth; for man looketh on the outward appearance, but the LORD looketh on the heart.** 8 Then Jesse called Abinadab, and made him pass before Samuel. **And he said, Neither hath the LORD chosen this.**
>
> 9 Then Jesse made Shammah to pass by. **And he said, Neither hath the LORD chosen this.** 10 Again, Jesse made seven of his sons to pass before Samuel. **And Samuel said unto Jesse, The LORD hath not chosen these.** 11 And Samuel said unto Jesse, Are here all thy children? **And he said, There**

remaineth yet the youngest, and,
behold, he keepeth the sheep. And
Samuel said unto Jesse, Send and
fetch him: for we will not sit down
till he come hither.

12 And he sent, and brought him in.
Now he was ruddy, and withal of a
beautiful countenance, and goodly
to look to. And the LORD said,
Arise, anoint him: for this is he. 13
Then Samuel took the horn of oil,
and anointed him in the midst of
his brethren: and the Spirit of the
LORD came upon David from that
day forward..."

It is very sad for someone to be rejected by God.
Therefore, when I read the above passage about
the rejection of Eliab and his other brothers, I
said, "Lord, why did you reject him because he
had the physical quality of a king?" He referred
me to the way and words that Eliab spoke to
David when David showed up on the battlefield
in **1 Samuel 17:28-30**:

"28 And Eliab his eldest brother heard
when he *(David)* spake unto the men;
and Eliab's anger was kindled against
David, and he said, **Why camest thou
down hither? and with whom hast thou
left those few sheep in the wilderness?
I know thy pride, and the naughtiness
of thine heart; for thou art come down
that thou mightest see the battle**.

29 And David said, **What have I now
done?** Is there not a cause? *30* And he
turned from him toward another, and
spake after the same manner…"

Remember that David was not yet old enough to be
a soldier but Eliab and the rest of his brothers were.
They were actually enlisted in Saul's army and were
in the battlefield with King Saul along with the rest
of the army of Israel. One day, Jesse their father sent
their youngest brother David to take food to them
and to check on how they were doing but when
Eliab saw David, the pride, arrogance, resentment
and jealousy in his heart were immediately revealed
in the way that he belittled David with his remarks.

When we look at Eliab's remarks to David in
the scriptures above, we can clearly see how they
reveal the quality of Eliab's heart. Also, when we
read **1 Chronicles 28:9** below, we can see King David
advising his son Solomon about **having a perfect
heart before God because God searches the hearts
of men.** God searched Eliab's heart and He saw that
his heart was not right and so He rejected him.

"…And thou, Solomon my son, know
thou the God of thy father, and serve
him with **a perfect heart** and **with a
willing mind**: for the LORD searcheth
all hearts, and understandeth all the
imaginations of the thoughts: if thou
seek him, he will be found of thee; but
if thou forsake him, he will cast thee
off forever."

On the other hand, when you look at David's reply to Eliab's accusations, you can see that Eliab had been putting him down in the past. It seems that Eliab had a habit of picking on David and of belittling him because David said to him in **1 Samuel 17:29:**

> **"What have I <u>now</u> done?** Is there not a cause?"

The truth of the matter is that David did not go to the battlefield on his own but was sent by their father to go and see how his older brothers were doing and to take them food. Therefore, his showing up on the battlefield was not out of pride but out of obedience to his father's instruction.

You can see that Eliab could not stand the sight of David as he says to him *(I'm paraphrasing)*, "I know the haughtiness of your heart, I know why you are here: **those few sheep; those little sheep that were given to you to care for, you have abandoned. Who have you left them with?**" He also was putting down David's profession as a shepherd and elevating himself, so in God's eye, he did not qualify because of his character flaw.

The interesting note about David's home life is that his father and his brothers probably thought that he was forgettable. To prove this point, we see that Jesse, David's father actually made all seven of David's older brothers to pass before the Prophet Samuel <u>twice</u> without once considering David as a potential candidate. The Prophet Samuel had to press Jesse concerning the number of children that he had before Jesse finally revealed to him that he had another son that was out in the field!

Although David's father and his brothers; in particular Eliab did not see him as even a candidate for kingship, **God chose him because of his demonstrated love for God and because of his trust in God.** God extended to him what He calls **"the sure mercies of David"** and called him **a man after His own heart that will do all his will.** David's choice as God's man is recorded in **Acts 13:22:**

> "And when he had removed him, he raised up unto them David to be their king; to whom also he gave testimony, and said, **I have found David the son of Jesse, a man after mine own heart, which shall fulfill all my will.**"

David may not have been much in the eyes of his father and the rest of his brothers but to God, he was the man that God was looking for as the custodian of the Abrahamic Covenant Blessings. By God's standards, David had done very well in choosing righteousness and in his love for God.

Do you remember what I have been saying throughout this book that God rewards whoever does well? The selection of David is a classic case of how God does it. One by one God tried all of Jesse's children and rejected them except for the one that reads Psalms and writes love songs to Him. Yes, the one that tells Him, "You are my Shepherd, I shall not want; You are able. When I am walking in the valley of the shadow of death, You are right there and I am not going to be afraid because You are with me. If a lion comes against me, You will help me kill it." In response, God says, "This is the man I have been looking for; a man after my own heart," so He chose David.

God did not love David more than all of Jesse's other children but because David earned it by his choice of righteousness, He gave the lineage of the Messiah to him. **Just as Judah earned the right to be the tribe of the Messiah by his choice of righteousness, David earned the right to be the person through whose loins the Messiah was going to come.** Therefore, God anointed David and He made David a promise that for all of eternity, **David will not cease to have a man on the throne of Israel.**

This is why when you look at **1 Kings 8:25**, you will see King Solomon (David's son) reminding God of His promise to his father David that the **Sceptre;** the rulership will not depart from the house of David. King David was from Bethlehem in the tribe of Judah so Solomon wanted God to make good on that promise to his father David:

> "Therefore now, LORD God of Israel, <u>keep with thy servant David my father</u> <u>that thou promised him, saying,</u> **There shall not fail thee a man in my sight to sit on the throne of Israel**; so that thy children take heed to their way, that they walk before me as thou hast walked before me."

True to God's Word that David will always have a man on the throne of Israel; the Messiah now sits on the throne of David and rules the earth from heaven! In other words, today, we call the Lord Jesus the Son of David and He sits on the throne of Israel and the throne over all the earth and He rules the earth from heaven. His kingdom is an everlasting kingdom that can never be destroyed. From heaven He is ruler of not just Israel anymore but the whole earth!

I am saying this to you because many Christians in the Church are trying to determine what tribe of Israel they are from and as you have seen for yourself, **it was carefully planned and supervised by God that the Messiah would come from the house of David in the tribe of Judah. <u>Therefore, anyone who was formerly a Gentile before becoming born again, cannot come from any other tribe in Israel but from the tribe of Judah</u>! We are grafted into Christ and we have put on Christ and Christ is from the house of David and from the tribe of Judah.**

As I stated earlier, there are currently some false teachings going on and certain Christians are being assigned to different tribes of Israel outside of the tribe of Judah. **False teachers are using astrological calculations to lineup certain tribes of Israel to the months of the year. They have also assigned the tribes of Israel to certain seasons and times of the year. Therefore, based on the month a Christian is born, these false teachers assign the Christian to the Jewish tribe that corresponds to that month and time of the year. How absurd!** I will address this later in detail in a chapter devoted just to it.

I say again that all Christians are from the tribe

of Judah because the Lord Jesus is from the tribe of Judah. As a matter of fact, Jesus is known as **the LION of the Tribe of Judah!** Therefore, I caution you not to let anyone tell you that since you were born in the spring, you are from the spring-time tribes of Israel or that you are from one of the summer-time tribes where the sun shines bright. **God did not use an astrological calculation to determine the tribe of the Messiah and you should not.** It was done by divine intelligence and God carefully supervised the plan over several generations. It took God thousands of years to fully manifest this plan in His Son Jesus.

In order to fully appreciate what God did for us in His Son Jesus, we have to take a look at the finished works of Christ next. Doing this will help to constantly remind us of the price that He paid for us which we cannot find in any of the other tribes of Israel but only in Him and in His tribe — Judah!

Chapter 8
Understanding the
Finished Works of Christ

Christ the True Seed of Abraham

The scriptures tell us in **Galatians 3:16** that **the promise that God made to Abraham that He was going to bless Abraham and his** <u>seed</u> **were actually made in Abraham to Christ.** In other words, the scripture says that **the seed that God was referring to was Christ and not to all of Abraham** <u>seeds</u> **as of many** (his numerous descendants). **This is why God had to make sure that Christ came from the tribe of Judah where He had placed the Scepter and from the house of David who had become the last custodian of the Scepter of ruler-ship**.

> **"Now to Abraham and his seed were the promises made.** <u>He saith not, And to seeds, as of many; but as of one,</u> **And to thy** <u>seed</u>**, which is Christ."**

It was also the reason why God had to make sure that the blessings were passed on according to His will so that Christ can come according to His plan. Christ came through David because when you study the genealogy of Christ, you will discover that both Mary and Joseph were from the house of David.

The Lord is the Root and the Offspring of David

The promise was made to David that the Messiah would come through him. Therefore, the Lord Jesus came on the screen as the **Son of David** and as our ransom sacrifice; the scapegoat to pay the price for everything evil that we have done to offend God. **He faithfully accomplished everything concerning our salvation and we call these the finished works of Christ.** When you look at the Lord Jesus' reference to Himself, you will see that He described Himself in an interesting way in **Revelation 22:16.**

This is a key point for those who are grafted into Christ to take note of because it will also help to keep many people from being misled today about their relationship to the tribes of Israel. The Lord Jesus **declared Himself as the ROOT and the OFFSPRING of DAVID:**

> "**I Jesus have sent mine angel to testify unto you these things** in the churches. I am the <u>root</u> and the <u>offspring of David,</u> <u>and the bright and morning star</u>."

As you can see, the Lord recognized Himself as being from the house of David and therefore, from the tribe of Judah. He did not claim any of the other tribes and if we are in Him, we cannot claim any other tribe also. He called Himself the ROOT of David and the OFFSPRING of David; meaning that He is the Creator (ROOT) of David as well as the Son of David! It is the root that bears the branches of a tree. This is clearly stated in the words of the Lord Jesus Himself in **John 15:4-6:**

> "Abide in me, and I in you. **As the branch cannot bear fruit of itself, except it abide in the vine; no more**

can ye, except ye abide in me. 5 <u>I am</u>
<u>the vine, ye are the branches:</u> He
that abideth in me, and I in him, the
same bringeth forth much fruit: <u>for</u>
<u>without me ye</u> <u>can do nothing.</u> 6 <u>If a</u>
<u>man abide not in</u> <u>me, he is cast forth</u>
<u>as a branch, and is withered; and men</u>
<u>gather them, and cast them into the</u>
<u>fire, and they are burned.</u>"

Without Him, there would be no David because
He created David. But for us that are born again,
the reference to the ROOT has even greater
significance as I will show you later in the next
chapter. Besides being the root, He is also the **Lion
of the Tribe of Judah.**

The Lord is the Lion of the Tribe of Judah

According to **Revelation 5:2-5**, when the
Apostle John looked into heaven and saw that
no man was worthy to open the seven seals of
judgment, he began to cry because nobody was
found worthy to execute judgment for God on
earth. In other words, no **man** *(an Adam)* was sinless
on earth, under the earth and in heaven to become
worthy to execute God's judgment on those who
have rebelled against God.

While he was crying, one of the elders spoke
to him about the Lord Jesus. The elder informed the
Apostle John that God actually has a **Lion** from the
tribe of Judah that is worthy to execute judgment
on earth for God. **Even to this day, the Lord Jesus
is the only man** *(the new Adam)* **that has lived on**

earth, under the earth and in heaven without ever having a single sin in His life. Therefore, He is worthy to open the seven seals and to execute God's judgment on all rebels:

> "And I saw a strong angel proclaiming with a loud voice, **Who is worthy to open the book, and to loose the seals thereof?** 3 <u>And no man in heaven, nor in earth, neither under the earth, was able to open the book, neither to look thereon.</u> 4 And I wept much, because no man was found worthy to open and to read the book, neither to look thereon. 5 And one of the elders saith unto me, Weep not: behold, the **Lion of the tribe of Juda**, the **Root of David**, hath prevailed to open the book, and to loose the seven seals thereof" (Revelation 5:2-5).

You can see one of the elders in heaven referring to the Lord as both the LION OF THE TRIBE OF JUDAH and as the ROOT OF DAVID! **Here you have it that both heaven and earth are in agreement that the Lord Jesus is both the Lion of the Tribe of Judah and the Root of David because the elder that spoke to John was in heaven.**

Again, what I want you to pay attention to right now is the word **Root of David** because you will need to remember it when we come to the next chapter that shows how we that are Gentiles were grafted into the **Jewish Root which is Christ**. A lot of the Jews in Jesus' day acknowledged Him as the **Son of David** whenever they pleaded for mercy and healing from Him. Below is an example in **Mark 10:47**:

> "And when he heard that it was Jesus of Nazareth, he began to cry out, and say, **Jesus, thou Son of David,** have mercy on me."

Continuing on in our discussion about the finished works of Christ, there is a key scripture that you need to be aware of concerning what the Lord did for us. We have heard that the Lord Jesus made atonement for our sins and this particular scripture in **Hebrews 9:13-15** tells us exactly how He did it. **I say again that we need to be aware of this so that we can appreciate what He did for us that we cannot find in any of the other tribes of Israel**:

> "For if the blood of bulls and of goats, and the ashes of an heifer sprinkling the unclean, sanctifieth to the purifying of the flesh: 14 **How much more shall the blood of Christ, who through the eternal Spirit offered himself without spot to God, purge your conscience from dead works to serve the living God?**
>
> 15 **And for this cause** *(reason)* **he is the mediator of the new testament, that by means of death, for the redemption of the transgressions that were under the first testament, they which are called might receive the promise of eternal inheritance.**"

God's righteous requirement is attained by obedience to His Word and His judgment against unrighteousness (rebellion against Him and His Word) is that the **"soul that sinneth, it shall die"** as stated in **Ezekiel 18:20.** Every human being came under the condemnation of death according to the word of the Lord concerning whoever sins. As a result, we all became guilty before God because God is so holy that He cannot look upon sin. Therefore, we all became separated from a God that loves us so much. Because of His love for us, He made a way for our sins to be washed away by the blood of His Son Jesus so that we can be restored to Him again.

<u>Through the workings of the Holy Spirit, the Lord Jesus went into the Most Holy place in heaven and personally presented His own blood to God the Father for the atonement of all of our sins.</u> **This is what you get when you receive God's salvation through Christ Jesus. The other tribes of Israel have no salvation plan for those who move outside of Christ into them.**

I say to you therefore that in the Lion of the tribe of Judah, you have the eternal inheritance (salvation) **that He bought for us with His blood and that God the Father watched carefully over in several generations to make sure that it was faithfully delivered according to His will to us.** This is why we are told in **Romans 10:4** that:

> **"For Christ is the end of the law for righteousness** <u>to everyone that believeth</u>.**"**

When you are in Christ, you do not need anything else to complete you or make you more Jewish or more of a child of God. We are truly partakers of God's covenant blessings. How did we that are Christians become partakers of this covenant inheritance with its eternal promises?

This question is the reason why I wanted you to make sure that you underlined the word **Root** in the scripture from **Revelation 22:16.** Keep it in mind because we are now going to take a look at a scripture that shows how we became partakers of the Abrahamic Covenant and its eternal blessings. I want you to see it for yourself in the next chapter.

Chapter 9
The Christians' Connection
to the Jewish Root

Christ as the Root

Remember what we read in the scriptures that Jesus is the ransom sacrifice for our sins and that He is the **Root of David**? He is not just the root of David, but He is also the root of Abraham because He is the creator of Abraham as well. **In short, He is the root of Israel and the tribes of Israel are the branches.** Therefore, we that have no natural Jewish heritage or lineage the Bible says have been grafted into the Jewish ROOT. **This is where the subtle heresy is coming in and where some people are bringing forth false teachings that Christians have been grafted into the 12 tribes of Israel.** This is a lie.

Where Christians Are Grafted Into

As a Christian, you are not grafted into the tribes of Israel but into the ROOT of Israel! There is a big difference between **the root** and **the branches**. Who is the root? Jesus is the root and He informed us in **John 15:4-6**, that the tribes of Israel are the branches. The scriptures by the Apostle Paul that we are about to see below tell us the same thing. The Jewish **Root** is Christ because He is the ROOT of both Abraham and David.

Therefore, I say again that in Christ, we who are Christians are grafted into the Jewish **root** and not into the **branches** which are the tribes. We remain in the ROOT only if we remain in Christ and we remain in the tribe of Judah which is the tribe that He represents. This is why the Apostle Paul said the following in **Romans 11:13-21:**

"For I speak to you **Gentiles**, inasmuch as I am the apostle of the Gentiles, I magnify mine office: 14 **If by any means I may provoke to emulation them which are my flesh** *(the Jews)*, **and might save some of them.** 15 For if the casting away of them be the reconciling of the world, what shall the receiving of them be, but life from the dead?

16 For if the firstfruit be holy, the lump is also holy: and if the **root** *(Christ)* be holy, so are the **branches** *(the tribes)*. 17 And if some of the **branches** *(tribes)* be broken off, and thou, being a wild olive tree *(the Gentiles)*, wert graffed in among them, and with them **partakest of the root** and fatness of the olive tree; 18 **Boast not against the branches** *(tribes)*. But if thou boast, **thou bearest not the root, but the root thee.**

19 Thou wilt say then, The branches *(tribes)* were broken off, that I might be graffed in. 20 **Well; because of unbelief** *(in Christ)* **they were broken off, and thou standest by faith.** Be not highminded, but fear: 21 **For if God spared not the natural branches** *(tribes)*, **take heed lest he also spare not thee.**"

As you can see, you were not grafted into the branches (tribes of Israel) **but into the Root which is Christ**. Some of the natural branches of the **Root** (Jewish tribes) were broken off because they did not believe in Christ. In other words, some of the tribes were broken off because of their unbelief but <u>they too will be re-grafted back into Root</u> (Christ) when they believe.

What you need to be aware of is that it is all about **Christ the Root** for the Jews and for the Gentiles because God wants us all to be in Christ; both Jew and Gentile! I will repeat again here what the Lord Jesus said in **John 15:1-5**. He said that He is the true vine and His Father is the husbandman and every **branch** in Him that does not bear fruit will be cast out:

> "**I am the true vine, and my Father is the husbandman**. 2 **Every branch in me that beareth not fruit he taketh away: and every branch that beareth fruit, he purgeth it, that it may bring forth more fruit**. 3 Now ye are clean through the word which I have spoken unto you.

> 4 Abide in me, and I in you. **As the branch cannot bear fruit of itself, except it abide in the vine; no more can ye, except ye abide in me**. 5 **I am the vine, ye are the branches: He that abideth in me, and I in him, the same bringeth forth much fruit: for without me ye can do nothing**."

As you can clearly see from the lips of the Lord, it is all

about Him the ROOT and not about the branches. We all have to stay connected to the Root (the true vine) if we are to be fruitful. This means that even the Jews today have to be re-grafted into Christ in order to bring forth fruit. **We are talking about the fruit of eternal life here and not material possessions.**

Some of the Branches are Still Broken Off

All Israel is not yet saved because some of the branches remain still broken off until they come to Christ. Not every tribe in the natural Israel is currently in Christ. **Therefore, there is going to be a reconciling of the Jews as they embrace God's plan of salvation in Christ but right now, God is still wooing them but He set His plan of salvation up in such a way that everyone has to believe in the finished works of Christ in order to come into His kingdom.**

As a result, even the natural branches now have to be saved by faith in Christ in order to share their eternity with Abraham, Isaac and Jacob! This is why Paul was saying that the natural branches need to be saved because many of the natural branches are still not aware that the time of the LAW is over. God's kingdom is now under the time of GRACE and everyone according to God's plan has to come into His Kingdom by grace through Christ; Jews and Gentiles alike.

In Christ Jesus, there is neither Jew nor Gentile because everybody has to believe what God did in His Son and confess it so that their sins can be erased forever. All Israel must now come to God through the

Lord Jesus Christ. There is no getting around Jesus the Christ to get to God according to the New Testament that is written with the blood of Jesus. He is now the only way to God. This is why Jesus said in **John 14:6:**

> "...I am the way, the truth, and the life: no man cometh unto the Father, but by me."

Based on what I have shared with you so far, you can now see that before a Christian goes and gets aligned with the natural branches (tribes) **that are not yet saved, the Christian has to make sure that he or she is not moving away from the Root because if you leave the Root, your Jewish connection is over.** God went into great lengths to make sure that we were well positioned in Christ and that we were properly grafted into Him for our salvation.

In essence, what I am saying and have been saying all along is that God's redemptive plan came through the lineage of Judah and the house of David in Christ Jesus and we cannot move away from it. The Apostle Paul was a man who loved the Jewish people and prayed fervently for the salvation of all Israel as we see in **Romans 10:1-4:**

> "Brethren, my heart's desire and prayer to God for Israel is, that they might be saved. 2 For I bear them record that they have a zeal of God, but not according to knowledge. 3 For they being ignorant of God's righteousness, and going about to establish their own righteousness,

> have not submitted themselves
> unto the righteousness of God. 4
> <u>For Christ is the end of the law
> for righteousness to everyone
> that believeth</u>."

This is of most importance to those who are going around looking to become members of the other tribes of Israel instead of remaining in the tribe of Judah. The Apostle Paul is saying here that those tribes need salvation. Again, you do not need to go outside of Christ to look for anything. He is sufficient for you in all things and the minute you go into another tribe, you leave the divine plan that God has carefully orchestrated to bring you to Him.

A Final Word to You about the False Teachings

What you should always remember is that the false teachings about the tribes of Israel do not take into account God's plan of salvation. They leave this important factor out altogether as they assign Christians to different tribes. You should never abandon the tribe of Judah to go into a tribe where there is no provision of salvation for you. **I have said several times already that not all the blessings that each son of Jacob** (the 12 tribes) **received are eternal. I also told you that the tribe of Judah is the only place where you can receive the eternal blessing of salvation or the blessing of eternal life with God after you leave this world.**

If after reading this book you still want to go back and pick a tribe outside of Judah such as the tribe of

Dan, then be aware that what you will have is bread (food for your stomach) all the days of your life while you are here on earth but after that, you will not have eternal life. Your only Jewish connection which is the Lord Jesus is not from the tribe of Dan.

As a human being whom God has given free-will and the ability to make choices in life, you are always free to pick a tribe that will "tickle your fancy" if that is what you want but at least, you will now be aware that tribes such Issachar, Zebulun, Dan, Gad, Asher, Naphtali to name a few, have no provision for your eternal salvation. No one died for you outside of the tribe of Judah to make atonement for your sin. Your salvation came strictly through the **LION of Tribe of Judah;** stay connected to the tribe of Judah and you will stay connected to Christ.

Therefore, whenever anyone tells you that you are from a tribe other than the tribe of Judah, just ask the person, "Who died for me in that tribe to connect me to God seeing that I am Gentile?" As I said before, if you step outside Jesus Christ; **the Root**, you do not have any connection to the Abrahamic Covenant Blessings which is what we are called to partake of in Christ.

Always remember that if you were born a Gentile, you do not have any Jewish connection without Christ, so be careful not to let fancy teachings make you to lose your salvation. When you hear these fancy teachings, discard them as people spreading ignorance and misinformed doctrines. You should not even give them a second thought. This is why the Bible tells us in **Matthew**

24:4 to be careful that we are not deceived.

"And Jesus answered and said unto them,
Take heed that no man deceive you."

My belief is that no one will stand before God on the Day of Judgment and claim that someone else deceived them because God made it our individual responsibility to take heed that we are not deceived. No one else is required to do it for us but we ourselves. Therefore, it is our job to test every doctrine that we hear with the Word of God in order to see if it stands the test of the Word of God. This is the only way that we can keep ourselves from being deceived because the Word of God helps us to discern what we are being told as well as the spirit behind it:

> "For the word of God is quick, and powerful, and sharper than any twoedged sword, piercing even to the dividing asunder of soul and spirit, and of the joints and marrow, **and is a discerner of the thoughts and intents of the heart**" (Hebrews 4:12).

Do not develop "itching ears" because "itching ears" are the products of lust and they lead to deception. They make you susceptible to false doctrines because you are craving to hear a new thing. According to **2 Timothy 4:3-4**, those who develop "itching ears" turn away from the truth of the Word of God unto fables:

> "For the time will come when they will not endure sound doctrine; but after their own lusts shall they heap to themselves teachers, **having itching**

ears; 4 **And they shall turn away their ears from the truth, and shall be turned unto fables."**

Also, any teaching that takes you out of Judah goes against the Lord's teaching about how we must get to the Father in heaven. He declared in **Matthew 8:10-12** that **faith in Him is now the only requirement to partaking of the Abrahamic Covenant Blessings. It is now a requirement for the Jews to come to God by faith through Christ instead of the works of the Law:**

"... Verily I say unto you, I have not found so great faith, no, not in Israel. *11* **And I say unto you, That many shall come from the east and west, and shall sit down with Abraham, and Isaac, and Jacob, in the kingdom of heaven.** *12* **But the children of the kingdom** *(the natural branches that refuse to be born again)* **shall be cast out into outer darkness:** there shall be weeping and gnashing of teeth."

In other words, under the Lord's New Testament today, even the Jews cannot get around Him to inherit the true blessings of Abraham. He said emphatically for all to hear that He is the only way to God in **John 14:6**:

"Jesus saith unto him, **I am the way, the truth, and the** life: **no man cometh unto the Father, but by me."**

You have seen for yourself that Jesus Christ is the

only way to God and that as a result, Israel itself needs to be saved in Christ. This is God's strategic plan in the New Testament and in His Son Jesus Christ. As I said earlier, it is not just the Gentiles that now need to confess Christ in order to receive salvation, but every single Jew also needs to confess that Jesus Christ is their Lord in order to be saved as well.

All who are born again are now the seed of Abraham with rights to the Abrahamic Covenant Blessings. This is a vital part of the essence of being grafted into Christ as we saw in the previous chapter. In Christ Jesus, we have become the "seed of Abraham" just as Isaac was when he was here on earth! The Apostle Paul spoke about this in **Galatians 4:28**:

> "**Now we, brethren, <u>as Isaac was, are</u> <u>the children of promise</u>**."

We need to know what the Apostle Paul is talking about when he said that as Isaac was so are we now the children of promise—the seed. How was Isaac? **As I showed you earlier, Isaac was both the recipient and the custodian of the Abrahamic Covenant Blessings from God because he inherited them from his father Abraham.** It was passed on from Isaac to Jacob and from Jacob to Judah and now it has come to us through Christ.

Isaac in his days was God's chosen one and today we are God's chosen ones in Christ because we believe in His finished works in Christ. Because we believed, our faith was counted unto us for righteousness just as Abraham believed and his faith was counted unto him for righteousness. You have to make sure that you watch over it and that you are very careful to guard it and not let a fancy preaching or teaching make you to lose your position in Christ.

We must all learn from the mistake of Esau who did not carefully safeguard his birth right but gave it away. As a result, he lost the privilege of being the one through whom God would have brought His Son into the earth. His brother Jacob that he gave the birth right to received that honor instead.

Chapter 10
Teaching About 144,000 in Revelation 7:7

I have carefully showed you throughout this book how God implemented His plan for our salvation through the generations and in particular; the introduction of the ransom principle. The RANSOM SACRIFICE OF THE LAMB began in the Garden of Eden and it was passed on through Seth, Abraham, Isaac, Jacob, Judah (as the chosen tribe) and finally through David and his house. It was not by accident that the Lord Jesus was sent to us by God the Father through the house of David. Again, God did not say, "eeny, meeny, miny, moe," Jesus would come from the tribe of Judah.

Even today, He does not say to us, "eeny, meeny, miny, moe," you are from Gad or "eeny, meeny, miny, moe," you are from the tribe of Issachar. It is not how He assigned Christ and those that believe in Him to the tribe of Judah. One of the **reasons why some people are spreading crazy teachings about Christians coming from other tribes of Israel outside of the tribe of Judah is because they misunderstand or misinterpret the scripture in Revelation 7 that talks about the "sealing of 144,000" from the 12 tribes of Israel**. Many people truly have a very warped understanding of what this scripture is talking about and as a result, they become deceived and they begin to deceive others.

The Truth about the 144,000
According **Revelation 7:4-8**, only a 144,000 (a

remnant) will be saved from the 12 tribes of the natural Israel. **Twelve thousand will be saved from each tribe which when you add them all up, comes to the famous 144,000.** According to the same scripture, **"multitudes and multitudes that cannot be numbered" will also be saved from all the other nations on the earth** but some people choose to ignore this aspect of the scripture passage as they carry on their crusade about the 144,000:

> "And I heard the number of them which were sealed: **and there were sealed an hundred and forty and four thousand** *(144,000)* **of all the tribes of the children of Israel.** 5 **Of the tribe of Juda** were sealed twelve thousand. **Of the tribe of Reuben** were sealed twelve thousand. **Of the tribe of Gad** were sealed twelve thousand.
>
> 6 **Of the tribe of Aser** were sealed twelve thousand. **Of the tribe of Nepthalim** were sealed twelve thousand. **Of the tribe of Manasses** were sealed twelve thousand. 7 **Of the tribe of Simeon** were sealed twelve thousand. **Of the tribe of Levi** were sealed twelve thousand. **Of the tribe of Issachar** were sealed twelve thousand.
>
> 8 **Of the tribe of Zebulun** were sealed twelve thousand. **Of the tribe of Joseph** were sealed twelve thousand. **Of the tribe of Benjamin** were sealed twelve thousand."

False Teachings about the 144,000

You have just read the famous passage about the 144,000 that many deceived people misinterprete and base their false teachings upon. The truth of the matter is that this passage in **Revelation 7:4-8** is telling us that only a remnant shall be saved from the nation of Israel because God will have His angels to seal 12 thousand people from each of the 12 tribes of Israel right before the wrath of God is poured out. This total number people that would be saved out of the natural Israel is very small when you think about the total number of people that are Jews on earth today.

What it is saying is that sealing only 12 thousand people from each Jewish tribe only adds up to 144,000 which is not much when you think about the entire Jewish people. **This is the emphasis or the point that the Apostle John was trying to make. It is meant to let the natural Israel know that they have to accept the Lord as their Messiah while they still can because only a very small number of people will be saved right before God's judgment.** The Apostle John immediately began to report that he also saw many more people being saved out of the other nations of the earth.

It is sad to see some of the evangelical ministers now getting caught up in the erroneous teachings about the 144,000. Christians are now being assigned to different tribes of Israel and outside of the tribe of Judah because of <u>the false belief that they will be sealed along with the 12 tribes as they become part of these tribes</u>. **In other words, they think that by belonging to the**

12 tribes of Israel, they will become part of the 144,000 that will be sealed!

This type of erroneous teaching about the 144,000 is one of the false doctrines that make the **Jehovah Witnesses** sect to stumble in the Word of God. I hate to see it also begin to now divide or shift Christians away from Christ, who is their Root to the other tribes that are not Judah; tribes that were not included in God's route of salvation for us.

Again, the Lord Jesus is the **Lion of the Tribe of Judah** and if you leave Judah and go to another tribe, you leave Jesus which is the **Root** that you were grafted into. You cannot be grafted into any other tribe in Israel because Christ is the only one that accomplished the works of our salvation and He is from the tribe of Judah. Outside of Him, you have no redemption.

Always remember that 144,000 is a very small number when you put into perspective that we are talking about the entire nation of Israel. The attempt to understand this scripture about the 144,000 that will be saved from all the tribes of Israel is one of the doctrines in which the Jehovah Witnesses group fell into the ditch concerning the Book of Revelation. They essentially believe that only 144,000 will be saved from the earth and go to heaven. They believe that the rest **of them who are not part of the 144,000 are not worthy to go to heaven but will remain here and inherit the earth.**

What is amusing about this belief by the Jehovah Witnesses is that they cannot point to any

deceased Jehovah Witness who is right now living on earth and inheriting it! If they are only meant to inherit the earth, why did they leave the earth and where are they right now? Their eyes have not yet been opened to see that no one of their deceased brethren is here on earth right now as an inheritor of the earth.

Again, according to the Jehovah Witnesses' teaching, only the sealed 144,000 will be eligible to go to heaven! This doctrine is nothing but a misinterpretation of scripture and it is the reason I tell the Jehovah Witnesses group whenever I encounter them to save this message for the tribes of Israel in the days of tribulation.

During the time of tribulation, they can then go throughout the four corners of Israel and preach it to the natural Jews that only 144,000 of them will be sealed from all the tribes. At that time, the message would be valid for the natural Jews but to us that are in Christ, it is a wrong message because according to the same passage in **Revelation 7:9-10**, John said:

> "**After this I beheld, and, lo, <u>a great multitude, which no man could number, of all nations, and kindreds, and people, and tongues</u>**, stood before the throne, and before the Lamb, clothed with white robes, and palms in their hands; 10 And cried with a loud voice, saying, Salvation to our God which sitteth upon the throne, and unto the Lamb."

This scripture above is in reference to us that were Gentiles before coming to Christ and as such were

not part of the natural Jews but came to Christ from all nations, tribes, tongues and people groups in the earth. This is where we come in because we are part of the **Root** which is Christ. We are believers in Jesus Christ and His finished works on the Cross. We were adopted into the Jewish **Root** in Christ and therefore, need to stay connected to that **Root** and not give it up.

In the days when the Lord was here on earth, He tried several times to make the children of Israel understand that He was their Messiah and as such the only protection that they had from their spiritual and physical enemies but they rejected Him. The Lord expressed His grief over the fact that they would not receive Him as their Messiah. He was very sorrowful over their rejection because by rejecting Him, they were rejecting the only protection that God gave them. He also knew that only a remnant of them would be saved on the last day.

The Lord said to them in **Matthew 23:37-39**, I had wanted to gather you just as a hen gathers her chicks under her wings but you will not let me. Therefore, He looked at them and wept for them saying, you will not let me protect you so now, your house is left desolate.

> "O Jerusalem, Jerusalem, thou that killest the prophets, and stonest them which are sent unto thee, **how often would I have gathered thy children together, even as a hen gathereth her chickens under her wings, and ye would not!** 38 **Behold, your house is left unto you desolate.** 39 For I say unto you, Ye shall not see me henceforth, till ye shall say, Blessed is he that cometh in the name of the Lord."

True to the Word of the Lord, Israel has gone through a lot of sufferings, hardships and wars intended to annihilate the Jewish people but God in His mercy has always fought for them. They are His people and we that are Christians share in their Root. In Christ Jesus, we have become the Seed of Abraham.

Danger of Abandoning Your Inheritance in the Tribe of Judah

A gentleman came to me and was very excited because he went to a Christian seminar or teaching session about the tribes of Israel. According to him, it was determined that he was from the tribe of Zebulun and this made him very happy. He proceeded to tell me how that he was now at peace because his Jewish connection was made clear to him.

I watched him display before me what I regarded as one of the highest 'display of ignorance' about Christ and about whom he now is in Christ. I was both angry at his ignorance and at the ignorance of a Christian minister who would teach this type of heresy to him. First, I asked him how it was determined that he was from Zebulun and he told me that they used an astrological calculation and his birth month to make the determination.

I looked at him squarely in the eye and said to him almost in anger, "Now that you are from the tribe of Zebulun, can you please tell me who died for you in the tribe of Zebulun to give you, who is a Gentile, a Jewish connection? Our Jesus is from the tribe of Judah and He is the only Jewish connection that we have, so how are you now grafted into another Jewish tribe if at all you are still grafted in?" His mouth was opened as he suddenly realized what his new Jewish tribe now makes him—unsaved! The truth is; no Jesus and the tribe of Judah, no salvation.

Not long after that, I met another person who also went to a similar teaching session about the tribes of Israel and it was also determined by some astrological calculation along with the month of his birth that he was from the tribe of Issachar. Oh, he was so happy because Issachar is known as the tribe that has wisdom concerning seasons and times. He informed me about how he has always been the type of person that seeks to understand seasons and times and in his summation, the teaching and its corresponding determination that Issachar was his true Jewish tribe was a powerful confirmation:

"And of the children of Issachar, which were men that had understanding of the times, to know what Israel ought to do; the heads of them were two hundred; and all their brethren were at their commandment" (1 Chronicles 12:32).

Again, I was amazed and angry at how some Christians can allow themselves to be so gullible and become deceived by false doctrines. I also asked him who died for him in the tribe of Issachar to give him a Jewish connection and who paid for his salvation in the tribe of Issachar and he too could not answer me. **I told him that some of the sons of Issachar had an anointing to discern seasons and times but the Lord Jesus through the Holy Spirit gives us understanding of all things.** The children of Issachar do not have one-third of what we have in Christ today when it comes to spiritual discernment. In Christ, we know far better than them.

Doctrines that Build Tabernacles around the Children of Issachar

There are those that have built a tabernacle on the one scripture concerning the children of Issachar having the knowledge of seasons and times. The scripture is a very valid scripture and it was a good thing that certain men of the tribe of Issachar had knowledge of seasons and times as well as what Israel ought to do but it was just one aspect of their God-given gifts.

For example, they do not remember Jacob's words that although Issachar had the strength of an ass, yet he became lazy and did not want to push himself to reach his potential; he chose a premature state of rest and thereby became a servant instead of a leader! Below is Jacob's blessing for Issachar in **Genesis 49:14-15** and as you can see, it is not a blessing but a reprimand.

> "**Issachar** is a strong ass couching down between two burdens: 15 **And he saw that rest was good,** and **the land that it was pleasant;** and **bowed his shoulder to bear,** and **became a servant unto tribute.**"

Building a tabernacle on one aspect of their gifts while ignoring other areas of their lives is not right. It will make us become like Peter in **Matthew 17:4**, who after witnessing Moses and Elijah in a conversation with the Lord on the Mount of Transfiguration, wanted to build three tabernacles; one for Jesus, one for Moses, and one for Elijah.

When you read that scripture, you will see how the Lord Jesus did not assign any importance to Peter's request by choosing not to answer it because He knew that Peter was speaking foolishness. Following the Lord Jesus' example, we too should ignore those who seek to make us build tabernacles around certain things that served to help us understand the generosity of God towards a certain people; an example of such is the anointing that was on certain men of Issachar to discern seasons and times. Apart from God's gift, the men of Issachar would not know anything; therefore, the praise and glory should rightfully go to God.

Peter did not have a full understanding of why the late Moses and the late Elijah appeared to the Lord Jesus and yet, he wanted to build a tabernacle for them. It was a premature move by Peter. Just like Peter, we are not called to build tabernacles around individuals or their accomplishments just because they were good. Our one and only foundation must always be Christ.

If the knowledge of seasons and times that certain of the children of Issachar had is your desire, I have good news for you and you do not have to come from the tribe of Issachar to operate in the knowledge of discerning seasons and times. In Christ, we have a much greater anointing to operate on a higher level than the one that the children of Issachar operated in. As a born again Christian who has the Holy Spirit dwelling in you, the Bible says in **1 John 2:20** that **you know all things!** In other words, you know more than any of the children of Issachar could have ever hoped to know:

"But **ye** have **an unction** *(Anointing)* **from the Holy One,** and **ye know all things.**"

The Holy Spirit reveals to us what we need to know at each given time and about anything. This daily dependence on the Holy Spirit to show us things goes beyond the knowledge of seasons and times. He gives us wisdom on what to do about anything that we request from Him. Again, this is a far better deal than the one that the children of Issachar had.

Also, we are told in **1 Corinthians 3:20-23** that **all things are ours.** Again, in Christ Jesus, the Holy Spirit teaches us whatever we have a need to know and He is not limited to seasons in His dealing with us. God has given us dominion and the right to possess all things as His heirs and as His joint-heirs with Christ.

"And again, The Lord knoweth the thoughts of the wise, that they are vain. 21 Therefore let no man glory in men. **For all things are yours**; 22 Whether Paul, or Apollos, or Cephas, **or the world, or life, or death, or things present, or things to come; all are yours**; 23 And ye are Christ's; and Christ is God's..."

I repeat again that Christ has given us an anointing that is greater than the anointing that the children of Issachar had. They only knew about seasons and times **but in Christ Jesus, we know all things by the power of the Holy Spirit.** The Holy Spirit can show us future events, He can forewarn us about impending danger, and He can guide us into all truth. It was a direct promise from the Lord Jesus in **John 16:13** that when the Holy Spirit comes, He will guide us into all truth and He will show us things to come:

> "**Howbeit when he, the Spirit of truth, is come, he will guide you into all truth**: for he shall not speak of himself; but whatsoever he shall hear, that shall he speak: **and he will shew you things to come.**"

As I stated in the first chapter of this book, I finally met someone who was told that she was from the tribe of Gad. Unlike the others, she was displeased with being assigned to the tribe of Gad because Gad's blessing was, **"Gad, a troop shall overcome him: but he shall overcome at the last"** (Genesis 49:19). This is not what we expect as a blessing when we petition God; this is not the type of blessing that you hope for.

Apart from lacking eternal value or provision of salvation, Jacob said in essence that Gad shall struggle most of the days of his life. His struggle could be physical adversaries, difficult situations and or just being plain unsuccessful most of his life. **The good news is that at the end, according Jacob, his circumstance or situations will not overcome him but that he will finally overcome them.**

As I looked at the blessing of Gad, I could understand why the lady was displeased with her assigned tribe. I also shared God's plan for our salvation with her and I told her how God carefully watched over the plan to bring it to pass through the tribe of Judah and the house of David. She too was shocked at how far she had allowed herself to be deceived and shifted away from Christ who is the Root of her salvation and who is the Lion of the Tribe of Judah.

The current teaching that is assigning Christians to tribes of Israel outside of the tribe of Judah is nothing but a fallacy; a subtle deception coming out of the pit of hell to make people lose their salvation without knowing it. Therefore, just like the Apostle Paul, **my question to Christians who are claiming other tribes of Israel instead of the tribe of Judah is?:**

> "O foolish Christians, who hath bewitched you that you should abandon your inheritance in Christ through the tribe of Judah to go to another tribe? Having began in Christ the Lion of the Tribe of Judah (the Root), are you now being saved through the very branches (tribes) that also need to be saved in and through Christ?
>
> Do you not know that when you step outside of Christ which is your Root to become part of a branch that you lose your inheritance in Christ and that you lose your Jewish connection altogether? Do you not know that leaving Judah means that you are no longer grafted into the **Root** which is Christ; the very LION of the Tribe of Judah?"

I want to again stress the point that we all have to be careful not to lose our salvation through some numerological teachings that use astrological calculations and some fabricated doctrines to try and deceive us. It is our duty to stay connected to the Root of Israel because we are not grafted into the branches (which are the tribes) but into the Root of Israel which is Christ. **According to the Apostle Paul, it is the root that bears the branches so why would anyone ever want to leave the root system to attach him or herself to the branches?**

My advice to you is let those who insist on dealing with the branches deal with the branches but you make sure that you are dealing with the Root. Stay connected to where God has connected you and do not seek to come from the branches. Always remember that the Lord Jesus, who is the Root, is greater than the branches. We love the branches but we are grafted into the root.

Chapter 11
Analysis of Jacob's Blessings Over the 12 Tribes

When the patriarch Jacob realized that it was time for him to depart from this world, he did what he saw his father do between him and his brother Esau—he passed on the blessings. He summoned his children to his bed side in **Genesis 49:1-2** saying:

> "...**Gather yourselves together, that I may tell you that** *which shall befall you in the last days.* 2 Gather yourselves together, and hear, ye sons of Jacob; and hearken unto Israel your father."

As we are going to see below and as I said in the earlier chapters, he blessed some of his children, he reprimanded some and he judged some. In other words, some of the children did not receive a blessing at all.

Jacob's Blessing for Reuben

> "**Reuben,** thou art my firstborn, my might, and the beginning of my strength, the excellency of dignity, and the excellency of power: 4 <u>**Unstable as water, thou shalt not excel;**</u> **because thou wentest up to thy father's bed; then defiledst thou it: he went up to my couch**" (Genesis 49:3-4).

As you can see, **Reuben** <u>received a curse instead of</u>

a blessing! Jacob told him that he was as unstable as water (lacks integrity) and that he will never excel. This means in essence that **Reuben will never do well in his life time**. What a judgment and a curse from a father to his son! Jacob took away Reuben's blessing and he gave it to Ephraim Joseph's last born.

To show how displeased he was with Reuben, Jacob adopted both sons of Joseph and he made Ephraim (Joseph's last born) his first born in the place of Reuben. Reuben lost his blessing and ended up with a curse.

Jacob's Blessing for Simeon and Levi

"Simeon and Levi are brethren; instruments of cruelty are in their habitations. 6 O my soul, come not thou into their secret; unto their assembly, mine honour, be not thou united: for in their anger they slew a man, and in their selfwill they digged down a wall. 7 Cursed be their anger, for it was fierce; and their wrath, for it was cruel: I will divide them in Jacob, and scatter them in Israel" (Genesis 49:5-7).

As you can see, Jacob was also very angry with both **Simeon and Levi**. As a result, they too did not receive any blessing from him. Just like Reuben their brother, Jacob judged both Simeon and Levi by saying that he will scatter them in Israel. Instead of blessing them, he remembered their wicked ways and how they killed the innocent because of their unrelenting anger. He actually scattered all the good things that would have come to Simeon and Levi to the other parts of Israel. This is why what Phinehas (the great grandson of Levi) did was of great value to the tribe of Levi. **In taking a stand for righteousness when the children of Israel were in the wilderness, he earned himself and his tribe the lineage of the Priesthood.**

As you saw above, Levi did not receive a blessing but a judgment from his father Jacob. Therefore, what Phinehas' his great grandson did was of extreme importance in getting the Levitical Priesthood blessing from the Lord. If not for Phinehas, Levi would not have received anything in terms of covenant blessings.

Jacob's Blessing for Judah

"Judah, thou art he whom thy brethren shall praise: thy hand shall be in the neck of thine enemies; **thy father's children shall bow down before thee.** 9 Judah is a lion's whelp: from the prey, my son, thou art gone up: he stooped down, he couched as a lion, and as an old lion; who shall rouse him up?

10 **The sceptre shall not depart from Judah, nor a lawgiver from between his feet, until Shiloh come; and unto him shall the gathering of the people be. 11 Binding his foal unto the vine, and his ass's colt unto the choice vine; he washed his garments in wine, and his clothes in the blood of grapes: 12 His eyes shall be**

red with wine, and his teeth white with milk" (Genesis 49:8-12).

Judah as you can see was highly favored and blessed by God through his father Jacob. He was given leadership over his brethren (scepter) which is to be passed on to the Messiah. None of the other tribes received this privilege. As a result, Judah was the only one positioned by God to be the lineage through which the Messiah would come.

Jacob's Blessing for Zebulun

> **"Zebulun shall dwell at the haven of the sea; and he shall be for an haven of ships; and his border shall be unto Zidon"** (Genesis 49:13).

Zebulun's blessing was just physical prosperity and expansion of territories. This is not a blessing that goes beyond the earth realm or into eternity. The good news is that he was not cursed but blessed.

Jacob's Blessing for Issachar

> **"Issachar is a strong ass couching down between two burdens: 15 And <u>he saw that rest was good,</u> and <u>the land that it was pleasant;</u> and <u>bowed his shoulder to bear,</u> and <u>became a servant unto tribute"</u>** (Genesis 49:14-15).

Jacob described **Issachar** as a lazy person who did not want to push himself to the point of dominance and as such became a servant to others. According to him, though Issachar was strong as an ass and tough enough to bear heavy burdens (to accomplish great things), yet, he became a servant. As I state before, because Issachar went into a state of premature rest, he was overcome and made a servant.

Most people do not know this about Issachar because all that they remember is that certain men of the tribe of Issachar understood seasons and times and they knew what Israel should do as recorded in the following scripture:

> **"And of the children of Issachar, which were men that had understanding of the times, to know what Israel ought to do; the heads of them were two hundred; and all their brethren were at their commandment"** (1 Chronicles 12:32).

The verse above reveals that certain ones in the tribe of Issachar developed the understanding of seasons and times. This was a direct gift from God to them because Jacob did not pronounce this blessing upon them. **Again, Jacob only reprimanded Issachar for being lazy and did not bless him.**

Jacob's Blessing for Dan

> **"Dan shall judge his people, as one of the tribes of Israel.** *17* **Dan shall be a serpent by the way, an adder in the path, that biteth the horse heels, so that his rider shall fall backward.** *18* **I have waited for thy salvation, O LORD"** (Genesis 49:16-18).

According to Jacob, **Dan** will be listed as one of the elders of Israel and shall be one of the judges in the land of Israel. Notwithstanding this, Jacob said that Dan has the ways of the serpent. A serpent bites you when you least expect and it seeks to paralyze its prey. From Jacob's description of Dan (a serpent and an adder), we can surmise that there was something about Dan that was subtle, conniving and deadly.

An adder is known for its venom and its ability to blend into the background so that it can strike without warning. Most bites from venomous serpents can result in fatality if not treated immediately. Remember what the Lord said to us in **Matthew 10:16**:

> "Behold, I send you forth as sheep in the midst of wolves: **be ye therefore wise as serpents, and harmless as doves**."

Dan's bites were not harmless according to Jacob. The tribe of Dan will receive eternal life when they believe the finished works of Christ.

Jacob's Blessing for Gad
> **"Gad, a troop shall overcome him: but he shall overcome at the last"** (Genesis 49:19).

According to Jacob, **Gad** shall basically spend his life in defeat but at the very end, he will succeed and have the victory. This speaks of a life of struggling with obstacles and unpleasant situations. The good news is that Gad will not remain in defeat but will eventually gain the victory over his enemies.

Jacob's Blessing for Asher

"Out of Asher his bread shall be fat, and he shall yield royal dainties" (Genesis 49:20).

Asher shall have abundance of provisions and food that is good enough for kings and queens. This is a very good blessing for physical and material prosperity but for us that seek eternal life, this is not enough. This tribe will receive eternal life only when they come to God through Christ.

Jacob's Blessing for Naphtali

"Naphtali is a hind let loose: he giveth goodly words" (Genesis 49:21).

Naphtali is not a lazy person but quick with his feet. He can run fast as a hind and his words are also pleasant. From this we can deduce that Naphtali was a peaceable man and spoke nice words to people. He was not cruel like Simeon and Levi.

Jacob's Blessing for Joseph

"Joseph is a fruitful bough, even a fruitful bough by a well; whose branches run over the wall: 23 The archers have sorely grieved him, and shot at him, and hated him: 24 But his bow abode in strength, and the arms of his hands were made strong by the hands of the mighty God of Jacob; (from thence is the shepherd, the stone of Israel (*meaning the God of Jacob*):

25 **Even by the God of thy father, who shall help thee; and by the Almighty, who shall bless thee with blessings of heaven above, blessings of the deep that lieth under, blessings of the breasts, and of the womb: 26 The blessings of thy father have prevailed above the blessings of my progenitors unto the utmost bound of the everlasting hills: they shall be on the head of Joseph, and on the crown of the head of him that was separate from his brethren"** (Genesis 49:22-26).

Joseph received the blessing of fruitfulness, strength and favor. According to his father Jacob, his land shall always be productive and be prosperous because the heavens will send him rain and the earth, and the sea will yield their abundance to him.

In essence, Joseph received the blessing of abundant prosperity and the physical blessings of his previous generations. Although Joseph received great prosperity blessings from his father, the lineage of the Messianic blessing was not given to him.

Jacob's Blessing for Benjamin
"Benjamin shall ravin as a wolf: in the morning he shall devour the prey, and at night he shall divide the spoil" (Genesis 49:27).

Benjamin will be a good hunter just like a wolf that hunts it prey at night and sit down to eat in the morning. In other words, Benjamin will know how to prepare his harvest in due season so that he shall not lack when harvest season is over. This blessing also has no eternal value attached to it.

Apart from the blessings that the 12 tribes of Israel received from the patriarch Jacob, they were also blessed by Moses in his days. What we need to remember as we look at these blessings is that it is Jacob's blessings that have the Abrahamic Covenant Blessings directly attached to it.

Moses blessed the tribes because they were all descendants of Abraham but the direct transference of the Abrahamic Covenant Blessings was by Jacob. We will now look at the blessings that Moses bestowed upon the tribes.

Chapter 12
Moses' Blessings Upon the 12 Tribes of Israel

As a leader, Moses blessed the 12 tribes of Israel before he departed out of this world. Though these blessings are valid and caused the recipients to be prosperous, they are however, not the same as the blessings that Isaac bestowed upon Jacob or that Jacob bestowed upon his 12 sons. They are essentially blessings of sustenance. They have no eternal provision outside of the earth realm for those who received them.

Also, although these blessings are addressing each of the 12 sons of Jacob, they were really for the tribes that the sons represented because at the time that Moses was pronouncing these blessings, both Jacob and all his 12 sons had been dead for many years.

Moses' Blessing for Reuben
"Let Reuben live, and not die; and let not his men be few" (Deuteronomy 33:6).

This blessing speaks to longevity of life and multiplication. This blessing can at least help **Reuben** counteract the curse that he received from his father Jacob. Jacob had said that Reuben was unstable as water and that he will not excel in life but here, Moses' blessing will open some doors for him to have a certain level of success and prosperity in life.

Moses' Blessing for Simeon

It is not recorded that Moses spoke a blessing over Simeon but some have argued that part of Reuben's blessings were meant for Simeon while others argue that part of Judah's blessings were meant for Simeon because Simeon comes after Ruben and before Judah in the birth order and in Moses' order of speech.

I do not agree with them because Reuben's blessing was spoken by Moses to Rueben just as Judah's blessing was spoken by him to Judah. Therefore, we have to agree with what is written in the Bible because Moses obviously skipped Simeon. We do not know if this was intentional or not. There is no recorded blessing by Moses to Simeon in the Bible. You can read Deut. 33 for yourself.

Moses' Blessing for Judah

"And this is the blessing of Judah: and he said, Hear, LORD, the voice of Judah, and bring him unto his people: let his hands be sufficient for him; and be thou an help to him from his enemies" (Deuteronomy 33:7).

Again, this blessing by Moses is for sustenance and for God's protection of **Judah**. He is to become satisfied by the work of his hands and Moses prayed for God to answer Judah's prayers and to help him in times of need.

Moses' Blessing for Levi

"And of Levi he said, Let thy Thummim

and thy Urim be with thy holy one, whom thou didst prove at Massah, and with whom thou didst strive at the waters of Meribah; 9 Who said unto his father and to his mother, I have not seen him; neither did he acknowledge his brethren, nor knew his own children: for they have observed thy word, and kept thy covenant. 10 They shall teach Jacob thy judgments, and Israel thy law: they shall put incense before thee, and whole burnt sacrifice upon thine altar.

11 Bless, LORD, his substance, and accept the work of his hands: smite through the loins of them that rise against him, and of them that hate him, that they rise not again" (Deuteronomy 33:8-11).

Moses confirms the Lord's Words that the **Levites** shall be the ones to minister at His altar. Remember that Moses was there when God made the Levites His priesthood tribe through Phinehas. As a result, they became the custodians of the **Thummim** and the **Urim.** Therefore, the Levites carried out the ordinances concerning worship, serving at the altar and teaching the people the difference between the holy and the unholy. They too received the blessing of sustenance and protection from Moses.

Moses' Blessing for Benjamin

"And of Benjamin he said, The beloved of the LORD shall dwell in safety by him; and the LORD shall cover him all the day long, and he shall dwell between his shoulders" (Deuteronomy 33:12).

Moses bestowed upon **Benjamin** the blessing of protection from Almighty God and for safety all the days of Benjamin's life.

Moses' Blessing for Joseph

"And of Joseph he said, Blessed of the LORD be his land, for the precious things of heaven, for the dew, and for the deep that coucheth beneath, 14 And for the precious fruits brought forth by the sun, and for the precious things put forth by the moon,

15 And for the chief things of the ancient mountains, and for the precious things of the lasting hills, 16 And for the precious things of the earth and fullness thereof, and for the good will of him that dwelt in the bush: let the blessing come upon the head of Joseph, and upon the top of the head of him that was separated from his brethren.

17 His glory is like the firstling of his bullock, and his horns are like the horns of unicorns: with them he shall push the people together to the ends of the earth: and they are the ten thousands of Ephraim, and they are the thousands of Manasseh" (Deuteronomy 33:13-17).

Here, Moses is repeating Jacob's blessing over **Joseph** almost word for word. Joseph's blessings are to make his horn (authority) strong like the horn of the unicorn so that he will continually overcome all those that rise up against him. **Ephraim and Manasseh** were to bring forth thousands and ten thousands of valiant men.

Moses' Blessing for Zebulun and Issachar

> "And of Zebulun he said, Rejoice, Zebulun, in thy going out; and, Issachar, in thy tents. 19 They shall call the people unto the mountain; there they shall offer sacrifices of righteousness: for they shall suck of the abundance of the seas, and of treasures hid in the sand" (Deuteronomy 33:18-19).

Moses blesses both **Zebulun** and **Issachar** in their tents and as well as in their going out and in their coming in. They are to have the treasures of the seas and of the land abundantly and they shall offer their sacrifices in righteousness. As you can see, this is essentially a blessing for sustenance with a divine aspect of sacrifices in righteousness.

Moses' Blessing for Gad

> "And of Gad he said, Blessed be he that enlargeth Gad: he dwelleth as a lion, and teareth the arm with the

crown of the head. 21 And he provided the first part for himself, because there, in a portion of the lawgiver, was he seated; and he came with the heads of the people, he executed the justice of the LORD, and his judgments with Israel" (Deuteronomy 33:20-21).

Moses basically helped **Gad** to walk in some form of a blessing that Gad did not fully receive from Jacob. His father Jacob had said that "a troop shall overcome" Gad but that Gad will "overcome at the very last." Here, Moses blesses all those who in the future will bless Gad and spoke to the fact that Gad will become one of the judges or leaders in the land of Israel.

Moses' Blessing for Dan
"And of Dan he said, Dan is a lion's whelp: he shall leap from Bashan" (Deuteronomy 33:22).

Moses called **Dan** a young lion or a baby lion (lion's whelp) but he shall be fast and agile even in foreign lands (Bashan). Remember that the children of Israel defeated Og king of Bashan? Dan is to be instrumental in foreign battles.

Moses' Blessing for Naphtali
"And of Naphtali he said, O Naphtali, satisfied with favour, and full with the blessing of the LORD: possess thou the west and the south" (Deuteronomy 33:23).

According to Moses' blessing, **Naphtali** is to enjoy tremendous favor of the Lord. God will bless him and he shall possess land to the west and to the south.

Moses' Blessing for Asher

"And of Asher he said, Let Asher be blessed with children; let him be acceptable to his brethren, and let him dip his foot in oil. 25 Thy shoes shall be iron and brass; and as thy days, so shall thy strength be" (Deuteronomy 33:24-25).

Moses blessed **Asher** with fertility and with feet that are as strong as iron and brass. One of the reasons that his feet will be strong is because they will be anointed (oil) by the Lord. Therefore, Asher shall have strength to face whatever each day brings him.

Conclusion

After reading this book, I hope that I have answered your question concerning the tribe of Israel that you are from. As you can see, the answer did not come from me but from the Word of God that is written plainly for all to see.

As I said in this book, it is our duty to test every spirit that speaks to us in order to make sure that it is from the Lord. We have to do the same thing with every new doctrine that we hear because God gave us the responsibility to "take heed that we are not deceived." Again, the only way that we can do this is to test all doctrines with God's written Word.

We cannot be like the Athenians in **Acts 17:18-21** that just loved to hear a new thing just for the sake of hearing a new thing. We must always remember that the new thing that we hear can be wrong even when it is coming from someone that we think has a proven track record as a solid minister.

> "Then certain philosophers of the Epicureans, and of the Stoicks, encountered him. And some said, What will this babbler say? other some, He seemeth to be a setter forth of strange gods: because he preached unto them Jesus, and the resurrection. *19* And they took him, and brought him unto Areopagus, saying, May we know what this new doctrine, whereof thou speakest, is?

20 <u>For thou bringest certain strange things to our ears: we would know therefore what these things mean.</u> *21* **(For all the Athenians and strangers which were there spent their time in nothing else, but either to tell, or to hear some new thing)."**

The Lord Jesus told us in **John 16:13** that the Holy Spirit will teach us all things and that He will guide us into all truth. We all need to rely on Him and on God's Word to help us understand what we see and what we hear. In other words, every Spirit-filled Christian should be able to call on the Holy Spirit to help him or her to use the Word of God to analyze what he or she sees or hears.

My final advice to you is to repeat what the Lord Jesus said to us all in **Matthew 24:4,** "take heed that no man deceives you."

— Dr. Mary J. Ogenaarekhua

About the Author

I am a born again Christian who believes in the preservation of human life and the sanctity of marriage as defined by the Bible. I also believe in living strictly by the Word of the Lord and nothing but the Word of the Lord. Below is the biographical information about me.

Biographical Information

Name: Prophetess Mary J. Ogenaarekhua, PhD (pronounced **Oge-nah-re-qua**).

Founder: Mary J. Ministries, Inc.

Educational Background: BA Communications-Journalism, Masters Degree in Public Administration and a PhD in Theology

Dr. Mary Justina Ogenaarekhua was born in Nigeria. She grew up in a Muslim home and attended Roman Catholic elementary and high school. The Lord miraculously raised Mary up from the dead when she took a fatal fall in her early years. Prophetess Mary is gifted with the ability to interpret visions and dreams, to hear the voice of the Lord, to discern spirits and to intercede as a mighty prayer warrior. She is also the Lord's scribe.

Dr. Mary operates in the gift of prophecy with the ability to see into the spiritual realm. God has opened Prophetess Mary's spiritual eyes to see His desire for His people. She's a teacher of the unadulterated Word of God; a true woman of God in rare spiritual form! She holds workshops and conferences as well as teaches and preaches on many topics including **deliverance, healing, visions and dreams, spiritual discernment, understanding the power of covenants, effective prayer, mentoring, leadership training and much more.** She conducts **evangelism and outdoor crusades internationally** with thousands in attendance.

Dr. Mary Justina Ogenaarekhua is the author of the following books:
  (1) **Unveiling the God-Mother.** This book is a biography of *Mary's death and resurrection experience* and her early years in Africa. It details the spiritual events that happened to her before she became a Christian and before she came to the United States. She also discusses some of the holidays that a lot of Christians celebrate ignorantly.

  (2) **Keys to Understanding Your Visions and Dreams: A Classroom Approach.** Prophetess Mary has an eagle's eye that sees far into the realm of the spirit. She was raised from the dead to instruct the body of Christ on how to walk in the realm of the spirit. In this book

about visions and dreams, she uses the Word of God to instruct the body of Christ on visions and dreams. She applies the first hand revelation knowledge that she learned from the Lord Himself. This book is a must read for everyone who dreams and everyone who sees visions.

(3) **A Teacher's Manual on Visions and Dreams.** This manual is a teaching tool for the average person, bishops, pastors, etc., the basic principles about visions and dreams, about sources of vision and dreams, about how to identify the sources of visions and dreams and how to analyze the contents of visions and dreams. It is meant to be used along with the above textbook on visions and dreams.

(4) **How to Discern and Expel Evil Spirits.** This is a very powerful book for all those who are called to the healing and deliverance ministry. In it, Dr. Mary teaches on the origin of evil spirits, how to discern and expel them and she answers the question: can a Christian have a demon? This is a foundational resource for all those who want to walk in great spiritual discernment.

(5) **A Teacher's Manual on Discerning and Expelling Evil Spirits.** This is a powerful teaching guide for those who are called to the healing and deliverance ministry. It is a teacher's tool with a step by step teaching on key principles about evil spirits, the origin of evil spirits and how to identify and expel evil

spirits. It is meant to be used along with the above textbook on how to discern and expel evil spirits.

(6) **How I Heard from God: The Power of Personal Prophesy.** Prophetess Mary outlines key principles concerning personal prophecy and she lays out a blue print of what to do with your personal prophetic words.

(7) **Effective Prayers for Various Situations: Volumes I and II.** In *Effective Prayers*, Prophetess Mary outlines and gives principles on how to pray effectively concerning various life situations. It contains prayers for almost every situation that a lot of Christians battle with. Many have given testimonies about the deliverance and blessings manifested in their lives as a result of praying these prayers.

(8) **Keys to Successful Mentoring Relationships.** In this book, Dr. Mary outlines the dynamics involved in a mentoring relationship and the actual steps and stages of mentoring. She also highlights the pitfalls to avoid.

(9) **A Workbook for Successful Mentoring.** This workbook is a powerful guide for all those who want to be mentored and those who desire to mentor others. It is a teacher/ student's valuable tool for teaching and practicing mentoring. It is meant to be used along with the above textbook on keys to successful mentoring relationships.

(10) Understanding the Power of Covenants. This book teaches on the power of covenants. Covenants impact our lives for good or for bad on a daily basis. This book allows us to learn about how God uses covenants, how the devil uses covenants and how God wants us to use covenants so that we can receive what He has for us and avoid the devil's attempts to use negative covenants to hinder us. Negative covenants can hinder a person's progress throughout life.

(11) Secrets About Writing and Publishing Your Book: What Other Publishers Will Not Tell You. This book is a powerful synopsis of what you need to know in order to write and get your book published and also how to position your book for mass marketing. It is designed to help all those who desire to write and market their books.

(12) The Agenda of the Few. This book is a call for the Church to get back to its God-given purpose for this country which is to reach all Americans for God. For too long now, the Church has been functioning as though it is only called to one political party –the Republican Party. The issues discussed in this book are meant to remind the reader that there are Ten Commandments in the Bible and that God can choose to address any of the commandments at any given time. Therefore, we must be willing to get the Church out of the box that we have placed it within the Republican Party and learn to seek God's will during each presidential election. He is the God of both the Republican and Democratic Parties.

(13) **The Agenda of the Masses.** Just like the **"Agenda of the Few"** that was written to the Christian Conservatives in the Republican Party, this book addresses what the Lord showed me that a lot of the Christians in the Democratic Party are doing that equally displeases Him. They have allowed a very large segment of the Church to be pulled away by "the agenda of the masses." In other words, they have bought into the ungodly doctrines, ideologies, beliefs, and political views of the masses to the point that now, their version of Christianity within the Democratic Party is essentially "anything goes."

Dr. Mary O. lives in Atlanta and is the founder of **Mary J. Ministries** and **To His Glory Publishing Company, Inc.** She is an ordained minister with a strong deliverance anointing. She has appeared on Trinity Broadcasting Network and other national television programs.

About Mary J. Ministries

Mary J. Ministries was founded by Dr. Mary J. Ogenaarekhua to equip and impart the anointing of God to the Body of Christ, for the purpose of impacting the whole world. Our goal is to help men, women, old and young to build relationships through Bible Studies, Community Outreach, Prayer Support, Caring Ministries, Teaching on Visions and Dreams, Discernment/Deliverance, Evangelism, Mentoring, Fellowship and Special Events.

As an ordained minister, Prophetess Mary O. teaches, trains and activates individuals to properly operate their prophetic gifts, discernment, deliverance and ministry outreach and interpretation of visions and dreams. Teachings provided by Prophetess Mary O. are inspired by God and are balanced biblical principles for the purpose of developing a spirit of excellence, wholeness and GODLY character.

Prophetess Mary O. is committed to helping the Body of Christ and those who do not yet know the Lord Jesus as their personal Savior to understand their God-given purpose. Mary J. Ministries regularly hosts classes, seminars, conferences and crusades in this nation as well as in Africa and Canada.

Contact Mary J. Ministries:
Phone: **770-458-7947**
Website: www.maryjministries.org

About To His Glory Publishing Co.

To His Glory Publishing Company, Inc. was also founded by Dr. Mary J. Ogenaarekhua to help writers become published authors. Our goal is to help new and established writers edit, publish and market their work for a reasonable cost.

To His Glory Publishing Company, Inc. offers one of the most cost efficient and stress- free ways of getting a manuscript published.

Books published by To His Glory Publishing Company will be made available in most of the major on-line bookstores like Amazon.com, Barnes & Noble.com, Books-a-million.com, etc.

Our authors receive a 40% royalty on the net sales of their books! Upon request, we submit our published books for buyers and distributors such as Wal-Mart, Family Christian Bookstores, drugstores, Publix and Kroger for review and purchase for their chains of stores.

We are a Christian organization with the sole purpose of bringing glory to the name of our Lord Jesus Christ. Therefore, we will not publish obscene or offensive materials.

To His Glory Publishing Company, Inc. reserves the right to reject any manuscript it deems obscene or offensive.

Contact To His Glory Publishing Co, Inc.
Phone: **770-458-7947**
Website: www.tohisglorypublishing.com

Bibliography

Ogenaarekhua, Mary J. How to Discern and Expel Evil Spirits. To His Glory Publishing Co., Lilburn, USA.

Ogenaarekhua, Mary J., Understanding the Power of Covenants. To His Glory Publishing Co., Lilburn, USA.

MARY J. MINISTRIES
463 Dogwood Drive, NW
Lilburn, GA 30047
Office 770-458-7947, Fax 770-458-7947

maryjministries@yahoo.com
www.maryjministries.org
Also check
www.tohisglorypublishing
for your publishing needs

Order Form for Books and CDs

Item	Description	Unit Price	Quantity	Total
Materials by Prophetess Mary J. Ogenaarekhua				
Bk1	Effective Prayers for Various Situations, Vol. I	$16.95		
Bk2	Effective Prayers for Various Situations, Vol. II	$18.95		
Bk3	A Daily Prayer Journal	$10.95		
Bk4	Unveiling the God-mother	$12.95		
Bk5	Keys to Understanding Your Visions and Dreams	$16.95		
Bk6	A Visions and Dreams Journal	$10.95		
Bk7	A Teacher's Manual on Visions and Dreams	$14.95		
Bk8	How to Discern and Expel Evil Spirits	$16.95		
Bk9	A Teachers Manual on Discerning and Expelling Evil Spirits	$14.95		
Bk10	How I Heard From God: The Power of Personal Prophecy	$12.95		
Bk11	Keys to a Successful Mentoring Relationship	$18.95		
Bk12	A Workbook for Successful Mentoring	$14.95		
Bk13	Understanding the Power of Covenant	$19.95		
Bk14	Secrets About Writing & Publishing Your Book	$18.95		
Bk15	The Agenda of the Few	$17.95		
Bk16	The Agenda of the Masses	$17.95		
CD Sets and DVDs				
Cd1	Visions and Dreams – 6 Part Series (Lessons 1-6)	$55.00		
Cd2	How to Discern & Expel Evil Spirits–6 Part Series (Lessons 1-6)	$55.00		
Cd3	Keys to Successful Mentoring Relationship–6 Part Series (Les 1-6)	$55.00		
DVD1	Dealing With the Strongman in Your Life	$18.00		
DVD2	Looking into the Spiritual Realm and Praying Effectively	$18.00		
DVD3	Understanding the Power of Covenants	$18.00		
DVD4	Understanding Your Visions and Dreams	$18.00		
DVD5	Spiritual Discernment	$18.00		

Shipping anywhere in Cont. US: Add $5 for First Item + $2 for Each Additional Item

**Please make check or money order
payable to Mary J. Ministries.**

Total of Products Ordered _____
Add 6% Sales Tax _____
Add Shipping & Handling _____
Total with Tax & Shipping _____

For Credit Card Payment *:

Name on Card: _____ Exp Date: _____

Card #:_____ Card Signature: _____
* We accept Visa and MasterCard

Ship Products To:

Name: _____

Address: _____

City: _____ State: _____ Zip:_____

Phone Number _____ Email Address: _____

All Sales Are Final – Contact To His Glory Publishing Co. for Current Prices at 770-458-7947 or tohisglorypublishing@yahoo.com

To His Glory Publishing

Let Us Publish Your Book

To His Glory Publishing Company will publish your book at the least expensive cost. We pay one of the highest royalties in the industry – 40%! We print on demand and place your book on the major online bookstores such a Amazon.com, Barnesandnoble.com, Bookamillion.com, etc.

Other Books by Dr. Mary J. Ogenaarekhua

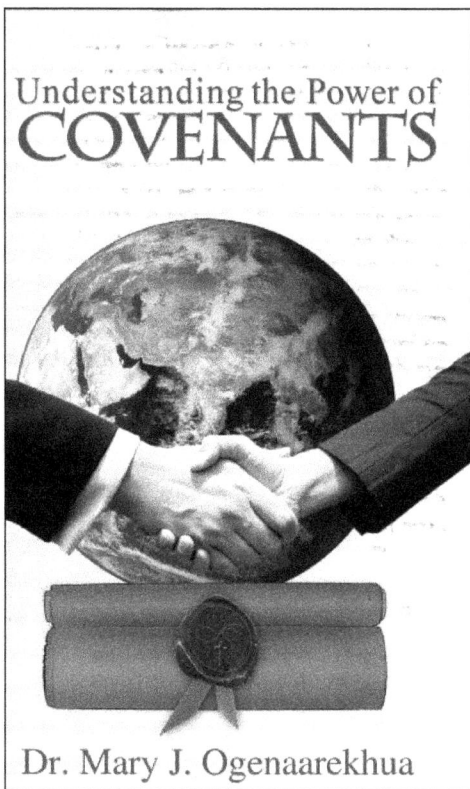

Understanding the Power of COVENANTS

Dr. Mary J. Ogenaarekhua

ISBN 978-0-9791566-8-7

ISBN 978-0-9821900-2-9

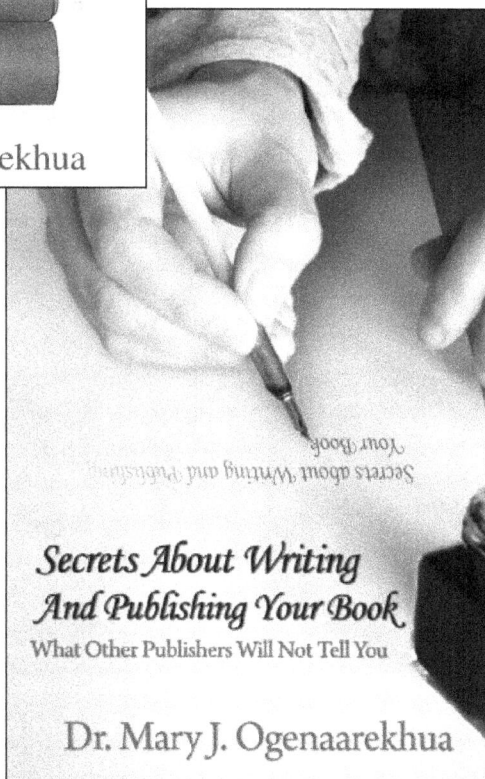

Secrets About Writing And Publishing Your Book

What Other Publishers Will Not Tell You

Dr. Mary J. Ogenaarekhua

Other Books by Dr. Mary J. Ogenaarekhua

ISBN 978-0-9774265-6-0

ISBN 978-0-9774265-9-1

Other Books by Dr. Mary J. Ogenaarekhua

KEYS TO UNDERSTANDING YOUR
VISIONS AND DREAMS

A CLASSROOM APPROACH

ISBN 978-0-9749802-1-8

MARY J. OGENAA
AUTHOR OF UNVEIL

ISBN 978-0-9749802-8-7

HOW TO DISCERN AND EXPEL
EVIL SPIRITS

PROPHETESS MARY J. OGENAAREKHUA
AUTHOR OF UNVEILING THE GOD-MOTHER

Other Books by Dr. Mary J. Ogenaarekhua

ISBN 978-0-9791566-6-3

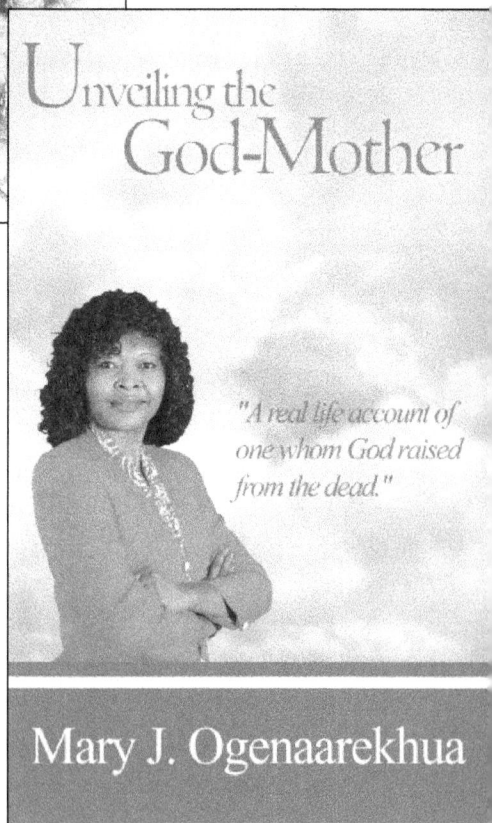

ISBN 978-1-5873628-0-4

Other Books by Dr. Mary J. Ogenaarekhua

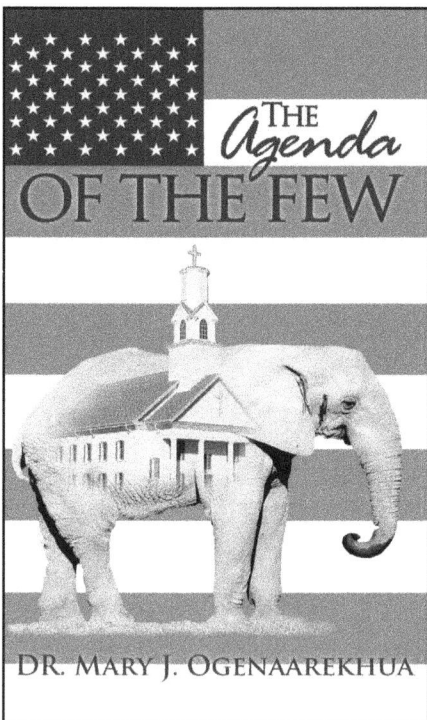

ISBN 978-0-9821900-1-2

ISBN 978-0-9821900-4-3